PUNK ROCK ENTREPRENEUR

RUNNING A BUSINESS
WITHOUT LOSING YOUR VALUES

CAROLINE MOORE

Microcosm Publishing
Portland, OR

PUNK ROCK ENTREPRENEUR
Running a Business Without Losing Your Values

All text is © Caroline Moore
This edition is © by Microcosm Publishing, 2016
Cover design by Caroline Moore
Book design by Joe Biel

First Printing, September 13, 2016

For a catalog, write
Microcosm Publishing
2752 N. Williams Ave
Portland, OR 97227
or visit MicrocosmPublishing.com

ISBN 978-1-62106-951-5
This is Microcosm #166

Distributed worldwide by Legato / Perseus and in the UK by Turnaround
This book was printed on post-consumer paper in the United States.

Global labor conditions are bad, and our roots in industrial Cleveland in the 70s and 80s made us appreciate the need to treat workers right. Therefore, our books are MADE IN THE USA.

Library of Congress Cataloging-in-Publication Data

Names: Moore, Caroline, 1983- author.
Title: Punk rock entrepreneur : running a business without losing your values
    / Caroline Moore.
Description: Portland, OR : Microcosm Publishing, 2016.
Identifiers: LCCN 2016000080 (print) | LCCN 2016002074 (ebook) | ISBN
    9781621069515 (pbk.) | ISBN 9781621061854 (pdf) | ISBN 9781621064145
    (epub) | ISBN 9781621061021 (mobi)
Subjects: LCSH: Punk rock music--Vocational guidance. | Punk culture.
Classification: LCC ML3795 .M67 2016 (print) | LCC ML3795 (ebook) | DDC
    781.66068--dc23
LC record available at http://lccn.loc.gov/2016000080

Contents

ATTITUDE

I can't remember the exact moment I decided to start a business. I have always done work on my own, outside my regular employment. Before I even graduated from college with my design degree, I had started picking up freelance work that I could use to pump up my portfolio for when I later applied to agencies. Despite a solid resume and a shiny new MFA, I couldn't overcome a saturated job market. Friends already working in the field reported receiving some 200 resumes for one job posting. There were simply far more designers than there were jobs, and I ended up working whatever day job I was offered. I cut out felt letters for hockey jerseys at a factory, provided tech support over the phone, and worked as a veterinary technician.

All the while, I sought out design clients—less to impress hypothetical agency types and more to do the work I really loved. It was work that I felt compelled to do even at the expense of sleep and social outings. Later, I started offering photography as a service, primarily wedding and portrait work, and eventually I realized that I needed a space online to show people what I did. I set up a basic website to display my photography and design work, and detail my services. It's been growing steadily ever since.

At the time, I didn't think of it as a business, though I was making money and logging as many hours as I did at my day job. It was just a sort of side-hustle thing that I was doing—something that I wanted to do, was skilled at, and had enough equipment to get started.

So I started. I grew up around people who were always working on projects. If a friend wanted to produce a zine, she would draw one up and distribute it. If she didn't have all the skills herself, she would collaborate with other kids—authors, artists, publishers—to get it made. Other friends wanted to go on tour, so they'd call venues, hook up with other bands, and ask their dads if they could borrow the old van. When I would ask my friends what made them do these things, they'd just shrug. *Because I wanted to* or *because I can* or *because I can't imagine any other way of living.* They couldn't picture a world in which they *didn't* approach life that way.

I grew up in a coal patch in southwestern Pennsylvania, which is not generally considered a hotbed of innovation and creativity. Still, I spent most of my time in high school and college around people who made things—music, venues, zines, art. If my friends had an idea, something that they wanted to put out into the world, they figured out the next steps to make it happen, and then they did it. I met people who believed in doing it yourself, in carving your own path, and in questioning established rules and systems. It's easy to hit an obstacle in your plan and stop there, to declare things to be impossible or, at the very least, just not doable at the moment. But punk kids, and successful entrepreneurs, don't jump straight to *no*. Instead of making excuses, they ask, *what do we have to do to get this done?*

The most important business lesson I learned from the DIY punk scene is that mindset. Punk kids have an attitude about, and a certain perspective on, the way the world works. I learned how to get things done, and quickly. I learned how to connect to people and how to be creative in a lot of ways—not only in the things I make but in getting my work out there. I learned that it's generally better to ask for forgiveness than permission, that is, if anyone even notices your bold move. These are the things I hope to impart.

You are going to run into obstacles. Whatever sort of business you're trying to create, whatever work it is that you want to do, will not be smooth sailing. How you handle those obstacles can make or break you. There are plenty of grim statistics about how many businesses fail in their first years and how few make it past five years. Failures generally boil down to a lack of planning (not enough people want what you're making, you've drastically underestimated your operating costs) or an inability to handle hardships when they arise. This attitude that I've picked up, thanks to hanging around DIY types, has fundamentally affected how I handle problems. Now, when something goes terribly wrong, my immediate reaction isn't *oh shit, we're boned* but *what can we do about this?*

Touring is an essential part of getting a band off the ground, so bands have gone to great lengths to make a tour happen. Not having a van is a pretty giant obstacle, but, again, people got creative and found workarounds. DOA opted to hitchhike from Canada to San Francisco and borrowed equipment for their first gig. DRI traded their PA for a van and sold everything that wasn't nailed down to cover gas money. Operation Ivy toured in a 1969 Chrysler Newport—a four-door car—for six weeks. Pat Spurgeon of Rogue Wave went on tour while waiting for a kidney transplant and had to do dialysis twice a day. Usually, this is done under extremely sterile conditions, but Pat had things to do. So, in the best-case scenarios, he'd get a motel room to himself. In the worst, he did his dialysis in a moving van. The band would roll up the windows, turn off the A/C, and put on surgical masks. It would have been easy for any of those bands to say *we can't do a tour*. But they didn't. Instead, they figured out a workaround to get where they wanted to go.

Some of these plans were better than others. The takeaway here isn't simply to jump without a net and hope for the best (nor is it to do dialysis in a moving van). It is, instead, to ask *what do I need and how do I get it?* If that's not a culture you've been immersed in, it can take some effort to change your thought process.

In addition to spending so much time around DIY types, I was also raised by people who made things happen. (My mother once applied for a job while barefoot, on a dare. They hired her.) Yet, I've still heard myself say *oh, I can't do that* without thinking it through. When I was accepted to give a conference talk in London, my kneejerk reaction was *oh, but I can't fly to London*. After a bit of time had passed, I thought, *why can't I fly to London? I have a passport, I'm not banned from that particular country, and I'm great at budgeting and planning trips*. Sometimes it takes a conscious effort to follow up that immediate negative reaction with *what do I need to make this work and how do I get it?* I did the research on what exactly it would cost, planned a way to pay for it, and organized my travel. I made a workable plan.

Get all the facts before you decide that you can't do something. *I can't* is an excellent excuse not to do scary things. It's vague, so you can't really argue with it. It sounds as though you've thought the situation through. *I can't* is just the first roadblock your brain throws out there when faced with a scary task. (It's right up there with *this is the way we've always done it*.) Usually, my counterargument is *what's the worst that could happen?* This is generally a rhetorical question, but considering what is the worst thing that could happen can help you to figure out exactly what is at stake. *I can't lose this job* is an immovable roadblock, but *I'm worried about how losing this job will affect my budget* is a concrete problem that you can begin to solve.

Alternately, you may realize that something is an extremely bad idea that you should run in the opposite direction of (i.e. *the worst thing that could happen is I fail at this stunt that I'm in no way prepared to perform and end up in a full-body cast*). The idea is not to jump straight to *no* but to carefully consider where saying *yes* might take you.

Another trap that keeps you from moving forward is comparing yourself to other people, especially people that you feel have it easier than you. Of course they can go on a three-month book tour, their parents pay their rent. There will always be people out there starting out with more privileges, more resources, more money, more support than you have. But there will also always be people who are doing it anyway with much less.

There are people who are far more hardcore than me in this regard, but because this is my book, you get my story. I have Lyme disease, which has ranged from nearly debilitating to kind-of-a-bummer. I've been working with Weapons of Mass Creation Fest since 2011, as a photographer and later a volunteer coordinator for the media crew. I was planning to do the same in 2012, but then I found out that I would have to get a PICC line placed four days before the fest. If you're unfamiliar, a PICC is a peripherally inserted central catheter—a tube inserted into an artery around your bicep so that you can shoot IV medications straight into your heart. It comes with a ton of terrifying warnings that mostly end with *and die*. If you get air in the line, you could have an embolism *and die*. If you get an infection, you could get sepsis *and die*. But I had worked at a veterinary clinic with my last PICC line, and I figured that a festival full of designers couldn't be any dirtier than that. I started thinking about how I could manage to photograph this festival for the weekend and still juggle my IV infusions.

I had to keep all the medication refrigerated during my three-hour drive to Cleveland, so I packed a cooler full of drugs and snacks, and made friends with the ice machine at the hotel. I had to do infusions every day, so, after spending the day shooting at the festival, I drove half an hour out to the Motel 6 and hung the IV bag off a floor lamp. One of the days ran really late, and I ended up having to do an infusion in the basement of Saigon Plaza, next to boxes of extra takeout menus and Christmas lights. Basements aren't generally a place you want to do semi-sterile procedures like IV infusions, but I've found less appropriate spaces (like an airport bathroom in Madrid, or a moving car). That summer, I shot two more festivals—with that same line. On my way to one, I met up with my dad for lunch. He said, "you know, most people in your situation just wouldn't work."

You can substitute my situation, Lyme Disease, for things that are more applicable to you. Most people with kids wouldn't give up their day job to freelance. Most people wouldn't start a business when they have a perfectly good job. Most people wouldn't sell their car to get a record pressed. Most people wouldn't.

In fact, most people would say that they can't, but that's not entirely the truth. There's a cost to everything—maybe it's money, it's time, or it's having your parents tell their friends that you're "in computers." It's important that you know what your plan is going to cost you. Often, this analysis reveals the things that you'll need to give up to get what you want. You should go into things with your eyes open. I didn't just hop in a car and hope for the best. I had to spend some time planning. I had to identify the things that I'd have to give up in order to make my plan work and decide whether I was okay with it. Maybe it turns out that you don't want it that badly, and that's fine. You're allowed to consider the sacrifices you'll have to make to grow your business and decide that it isn't for you. But you don't want to have that realization after you've quit your job, taken out a loan, or signed a lease on a storefront. Doing research and planning is a crucial step, so that you don't have to learn the hard way that it isn't what you want.

Once you've decided you're in it, a great first step in your plan is figuring out your MVP. If you don't spend a lot of time around start-ups, MVP stands for Minimum Viable Product. The idea is to make something that has just the core features that are necessary, and nothing more. No bells and whistles, just a solid, functioning thing. You create this MVP and ship it to a small audience, and then you get feedback to improve your next version. It's an iterative process in which you generate an idea, prototype it, present it, analyze the responses you collect, and plan from there. This strategy helps you avoid spending years creating software only to find that no one needs or wants it.

The concept is familiar to the punk scene, though I've never heard a musician use the term "MVP." In punk, it feels more like *what's the least we can get away with?* (Sometimes, one-minute songs are all you need.) Using the MVP process, musicians write and practice songs, play them live at a show, and find out what works and what doesn't before going into the studio to record. Basement shows are a great example of an MVP. If you don't have a venue, find a space with electricity. Bands have played in delis, in laundromats, in back rooms of warehouses, in parking lots, in churches, in VFW halls, and on people's lawns. Flatline, a small-town band, has played shows in a three-car garage, in a field, and in a Taco Bell parking lot. You may not be able to book traditional venues, or you may live somewhere that doesn't have traditional venues, especially for smaller bands.

I went to school for design, and took nearly every studio art class that was offered. I learned a lot about what artists call ad-hoc spaces—ad hoc is Latin for "for this." It's a makeshift solution that is designed to fulfill an immediate need. There was no gallery on campus, so we had to find a nearby space that we could modify into a gallery. Whatever you're calling your process, what you're really doing is determining those core features that are necessary to your product, your service, your event. And once you determine those core features, then you start to get creative about achieving them.

When The Replacements released *Stink*, in 1982, they couldn't afford to have the album jackets professionally printed. So they carved the word "Stink" into a potato, inked it, and hand stamped each one. Maybe you can't afford to print an album cover, but you can buy a potato and some stamp ink for well under $5. Figuring out your MVP gives you a very clear idea of what you do—and don't—need to make your business work.

> "Punk rock is really all about trimming the fat and getting rid of what you don't need. I'm a full-time musician today and do 150-200 shows a year because of what I learned in the punk scene. A lot of musicians are crying today that there's not money in music. Maybe you can't afford a jet and Lamborghini, but I have a house and live pretty comfortably, and I never went into music for those other things in the first place. When we don't need tour buses, hotels, high-end food, cocaine, strippers, and fancy rides, we don't use them, and that means money saved. It's all economics, money in and money out. I'd rather be able to live my dream punk-rock style than be on a sinking ship of debt trying to be Guns and Roses in '89." —Adam Joad, Scattered Hamlet

When I started to ramp up the photography end of my business, I spent a lot of time reading blogs and articles about all the start-up costs I'd need to cover: *You're going to need a serious computer with this kind of processor and this much RAM. You need this software, that lens, this camera system. Get a studio, a big one, with a real office—you'll need that. And supplies—we're running a business here, you'll need thousands of dollars in overhead.*

Had I followed any of that advice, I might still have a successful business, but I would be buried under a gigantic mountain of debt.

When I officially started my business, and filed all the paperwork to make it nice and legal, I had a three-year-old laptop with Photoshop CS3 and the tiniest desk known to man set up in a corner of my bedroom. I had a consumer-level Nikon camera (the cheapest DSLR they offered at the time) with three prime lenses. That was it. I determined that this was my MVP—I had a camera system that could cover anything, and I had a computer that, while slow as hell, could edit those photos. It cost me time, but when I started, I had much more time than I had money.

Eventually, I started making money. I posted client and personal work to the site, and updated the blog. People started finding me, and later, recommending me to their friends. I started investing some of the money I was making back into the business. I've upgraded the camera system more than once since then, and I've purchased software that isn't strictly necessary, but it saves me a huge amount of time. Nearly a decade in, I still don't have some of the things that those articles told me I couldn't start a business without. The DIY attitude helped me to work through these processes—identify what a project will cost, the least that I'll need to get it off the ground, and how I can realistically go about supporting it. If you take the time to get creative and really think about all your options to produce something, often it's a lot less expensive or a lot easier to achieve than you might have thought.

The next time an obstacle or an opportunity presents itself, and your immediate thought is *I can't do that*, try to follow it up with . . . *but what if I could?* In the end, you may still find that your initial response is correct, that a project just won't work out. But you may find yourself with a plan that allows you to overcome that obstacle or achieve that goal, and that's certainly worth the time it takes you to ask a few questions.

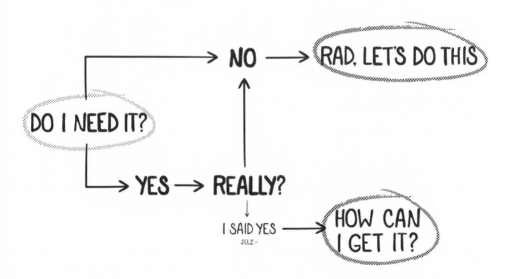

BUILDING A NETWORK

Networking is often met with resistance. Understandably, most people associate that word with a roomful of vaguely intoxicated people in suits, passing out business cards to other people who want only to pass out their own business cards. That sounds horribly unpleasant, but so many people starting out in business view it as a necessary evil. Aside from being boring as hell, it's also a really inefficient way to connect with people.

When I started out, I researched strategies and advice for networking. Many suggest setting a goal for how many cards you'll pass out at an event, maybe 25 or 50. Let's say I'm feeling really productive, so I aim for 50. (We're gonna do some math here, stay with me.) At a three-hour event, that means I get to spend just shy of four minutes with each person I'm handing a card to. That barely gives me enough time to introduce myself and explain what I do, and then I've got to be off to "meet" someone else, or I won't make my quota for the night. Did you have a project that's really interesting? Who cares? I have cards to pass out.

Even if I decrease my quota to 25 cards in that time frame, I increase my interaction time to barely seven minutes. This is also assuming that I stick to my plan the entire time. *Put down that coffee. Coffee is for closers. You don't need to eat, we're here to pass out cards.* In seven minutes, I can do a pretty solid introduction and maybe ask the other person what he does, as long as he's not long-winded. *Yes, you make blankets for orphans. Tick tock buddy, I don't have all day.*

So you may have completed your arbitrary goal of handing out all those business cards, but you've failed to inspire anyone to follow up on it. They don't know you, or care about you, or likely even remember exactly what it is that you do, aside from abruptly leaving conversations. If your goal is simply to get your information in front of some strangers, you'd be better served to burst in and fling cards into the air like confetti. At least they'd be likely to remember that.

If you want to build a network, the goal is to connect with people. And it's difficult, maybe impossible, to make a real connection with and a lasting impression on people in under ten minutes. Plus, not only are you failing to make an impression on them but you're missing out on getting to know them and what they do. Maybe the two of you would have really hit it off over your shared love of Magic the Gathering or building model trebuchets, but you'll never know that if you flit from one forced interaction to the next. Pretty much every good thing that's happened to me, business or otherwise, has been because of relationships with people. That's all networking is. It's not an elevator pitch and here's-my-business-card. You're building relationships with people. Go all in with it. Introduce people that you know have common interests and goals, and others will start doing the same for you. Grow those relationships over time, meet more people, and build relationships with them to expand your network. If you approach it with that kind of mindset, networking doesn't have to be horrible or ineffective. I grew up with a very different idea of how networking functions, and it involved a lot more couch-surfing.

Building a network is a huge deal if you're a touring band. You don't have the usual support system that you do at home, and you're frequently forced to rely on the kindness of strangers. You're relying on these people you meet to bail you out, to give you a place to stay or a show to play when yours gets cancelled at the last minute. It takes all different kinds of people to keep you going on the road. But once you've been touring awhile, you've met and built relationships with all kinds of people—people in bands, photographers and designers and promoters, people who will let you crash on their floor, kids that run venues and labels out of back rooms. Now you know a band in Idaho that can open for you, and you can return the favor when they're in town. You know someone who works at a local paper that can review your show. You've met a great designer who will work with you on your next record, and you've met kids that will feed you when you're in town. You've built a network of people, and you take care of each other.

Henry Rollins talks about building a network in a documentary called *Punk's Not Dead*. He didn't say "and this is how we built a network," but it is. Back before you could pre-order anything you wanted through the Internet and get an album without ever leaving your house, a lot of bands functioned through mail order. You would send away for a 7" in the mail, and generally someone in the band, rather than a distributor, filled the orders. The bassist would send you your record, and maybe he'd mention that the band would be coming through your town soon and ask if they could crash with you. Then the next thing you know, some guy named Joey Shithead is at your house. If you're in a band too, the next time Joey Shithead is in town, he'll ask you to open for his band. I'm paraphrasing, but the gist is that you're not just cold-calling a touring band to see if you can be on the bill. You're building an actual relationship with another person. It's a relationship that's not a one-way street, and you help each other out. Being nice is a pretty amazing force when it comes to getting things made.

"One of the first houses I bought was a duplex, and I lived in half of it and rented the other half. I got to know the other people fairly well and still saw them when I moved to my own house. They had been behind on their rent, but I was working with them because they had been there a few years and never gave me problems. Then their dog got hit by a car. They called me and asked to borrow money so the dog could have surgery and be saved. They probably owed me two months rent at the time, but I loaned them the money. I mean, it's a dog, right? They paid me back in about a month, and were caught up with their rent within a month after that. (This is a very, very rare case in the real-estate business.) Save dog = feel good and get paid. Everyone wins." —Curtis Sproul, property manager

Being interested is an amazing force as well. So many of my professional relationships have originated from contacting people just to tell them that I think what they're doing is cool. I want them to know that. I never expect anything to come of that, but sometimes it does. Most often, those bands and organizations hire me to take photos. They circulate those photos among their friends, and I get to be the person known for photos. People see me around at shows with my giant camera, but they also see me support my scene—I buy merch, I help promote events, I support local bands and organizations. I've met people through paid and volunteer work, through collaborations with other artists, at industry events, and in completely unrelated places. When you think of networking as a thing you set out to do at sanctioned events only, you limit the kind of people that you'll meet. But when you view networking as just getting to know other interesting people, you're always doing it naturally wherever you go. And opportunities pop up in unexpected places.

In fact, my volunteering started a ball rolling that resulted in this book.

Part design conference, part music festival, part art show, Weapons of Mass Creation Fest is a yearly festival in Cleveland that brings creatives together. I'd heard about the first one a few weeks after the event had already happened, so I kept an eye out for updates the following year. I knew I wanted to attend, but it seemed like something I'd also really like to be part of. I asked Jeff Finley, who organized the event, if he had any need for a photographer, and he was happy to have the help. I spent my weekend photographing every speaker on the lineup. I met some great people, added some shots to my portfolio, and apparently made an impression on the folks running the festival. The following year, the festival expanded, like these things tend to. Instead of having to play at the local bar, bands had a space with indoor and outdoor stages that allowed music all day. Jeff asked if I'd be willing to organize more volunteers to cover the weekend, to make sure we got photos of everything. With simultaneous events, I couldn't attend every talk and show. I agreed and became part of the official staff for the festival. I've coordinated that crew every year since.

During my third year, on top of photographing as much as I could and organizing the volunteers, I also had an idea for a talk called "How Punk Rock Made Me a Better Entrepreneur." I had a good read on the crowd there, and on what sort of presentation would go over well. I later turned that talk into this book you're reading. I've met really wonderful people as a result of volunteering, some of which I've ended up collaborating with or doing work for. I was able to photograph some pretty unique events, and to learn a little more about what it takes to organize media coverage. I got to talk to a roomful of people who approached me after to share their own experiences. This book exists because I offered to volunteer for a weekend in 2011 because I felt that WMC was doing something good for the industry. I've had some absolutely amazing experiences thanks to getting involved with a community.

"The passionate community in the DIY punk scene always sort of felt like a family. Of course, I always felt like an outcast no matter what, which is why I started Weapons of Mass Creation Fest. I felt like if these kids could start their own fest, then I could as well. Just by watching them, I felt like I could do it. I wanted to create the same sort of intimate vibe at WMC Fest, the one I felt going to Berea Fest or DIT Fest.

I always felt a connection with the outcasts, the emo kids, the punks, the goths, the ones nobody else liked because they were too different. While I wasn't one to don black eyeliner, I somehow related. People wore their hearts on their sleeve, and that's how I live my life. Music inspired me to work for myself. So much of my early work was t-shirt designs, posters, and band logos. I felt like I was part of the scene in my own way. I felt at home. Like this was meant for me."

—Jeff Finley, founder of WMC Fest

The success stories stick, but sometimes nothing comes of donating your time. I volunteered with Flashbus when it came through town, because it meant I got to attend the seminar for free. It sounds dirty, but it was actually a tour in which Joe McNally and David Hobby were teaching their different lighting methods, and their chosen mode of travel was a huge bus. I got to meet them both and chat with some great photographers, and it was a good day despite the 5 a.m. call time. But I didn't end up landing a gig as Joe's assistant, hiking across the Serengeti for *National Geographic*, or meeting a huge client that loved my work. I did learn some useful stuff and met a few other photographers that I still keep in touch with.

You never know which connections might turn into something. If the only outcome that appeals to you is the one in which you're getting something from the other person, volunteering is probably not how you should invest your time and energy. If you're applying for a job or bidding for a project, then of course you're expecting a specific thing from the other person. Volunteering—getting involved in a community—should be its own reward, and that's the only way it's going to help you build your network. Do you really want to spend your free time with people that you don't like, working on things you don't care about, just because you might get something out of it? If you do manage to land a gig out of it or sell someone on the product you're making, then congratulations! You get to spend even more time and energy with people you don't like, working on things that you don't care about. The upshot to working within a community that you honestly care about (aside from its being fulfilling in and of itself) is that the connections you make are with people you'd actually *want* to work with.

You can fortify your network by facilitating new connections for other people. I'm involved in my industry, which means I know a lot of people who do work that's similar to what I do. I have photographer friends that shoot different styles and subjects than I do. I know designers that work in different specialties, so I get to be a great referral system for them. I don't really draw comics, but I know someone who does. I don't do corporate-event photography, but I know someone who does. So when I meet someone who's looking for that kind of work, I get to share that resource and connect those people.

It takes all different kinds of people to keep a business running. I'm pro-DIY, but there are still things that I simply have to delegate. I can't possibly be an expert at everything. Part of managing my time well means recognizing my strengths, what is necessary for me to do myself, and what I can and should be handing off to someone else. It can be hard to pass off parts of your business. You like to think that you're irreplaceable, and for some aspects of your business, you absolutely are. No one else would do it the same way. But there are other aspects of your business that could be done by someone else just as well or better. I'm technically able to screen-print a shirt, but I have friends that are amazing at it. The benefit to building up your network is that you meet people who are amazing at things that you're just sort of okay at, and you can trust that they'll get you a quality product.

At this point, I know a vendor for nearly anything a client could want. You want that printed on a t-shirt? Coffee mug? Billboard? Hockey puck? I know a girl. And if I don't know someone, someone that I know has a go-to person. When I shoot a show or an event out of state, I have a long list of people who will let me crash on their couch. When people approach me about work that I don't really do, I have wonderful contacts whom I can refer. I have a large network of people, and I've built it in exactly the way that I outlined—by taking a genuine interest in people I meet, building a relationship, and helping them out when I can. I support my scene, I give advice to other photographers and designers when they ask, I recommend these people to my friends, and I've taken in some couch-surfers myself. I invest my time in communities that I honestly care about. When you move past *what do I need?* and onto the *how do I get it?* your network is an invaluable resource to making it happen.

There used to be an annual booklet that *Maximum Rocknroll* put out, called *Book Your Own Fucking Life*. It's no longer in print, but it lives on as a website. It was effectively a cheat sheet for planning a tour, before emailing was really a thing, when venues didn't have websites and dinosaurs roamed the earth. There were sections for promoters, for other bands in that area, and for places that would let you play, all broken down by region. But the thing that made it work was that people shared their connections. The booklet took that concept—connecting people to each other—and collected all those resources in one place. People would write in to update venues that closed, or new ones that popped up, or phone numbers that were disconnected. People helped to make that resource better, because others had taken the time to do the same for them.

And they certainly weren't the only ones doing it—*Rock Scene, Punk Globe, Cometbus*—a million other small-town zines relied on people to contribute scene reports on bands they cared about. *Maximum Rocknroll* featured scene reports from all over, and that's how a lot of people got exposed to new bands. Officially sanctioned meetups are one way to meet people who do the kind of work you do, but if you're paying attention, there are plenty of other ways to find them. I used to read the thank-you sections of liner notes on albums to find new bands. Now I check photo credits in newspapers and magazines to find photographers who are doing cool work.

When people need something done, they come to the people they know, so it's a matter of you being a person they know. The best way to do that is to show up for them. Get involved.

Friends know that I do concert photography because they see me doing it, and they see me doing it because I love live music. When I go to industry events, whether it's a designer meetup or a basement show, I meet people. I'm certainly not racking up twenty-five or fifty connections, but I do genuinely connect with somewhere between one and five people when I go. And after the event, I keep up with them. When I spend more than five minutes with them, I get to know what they do, what projects they're working on, and what they're into. Because of this, I've never had trouble finding a local vendor for anything that I need to have produced. While I do a lot of design work for people, I'm not generally putting out the finished product, so I need to know printers, and screen printers, and woodworkers, and button makers, and people who own laser cutters. I delegate all that to people who make their living being great at their craft. Not only do I get to support local businesses by sending work their way but I become a good resource for others, and I promote their businesses any chance I get. You rely on the people you meet to help you out. The flip side is that you're also expected to be a resource, to help others out, so that you're building a community and not taking advantage of other people's kindness. It's less about stuffy networking events, more about couch-surfing and rides to the airport. Sometimes business relationships turn into friends, and sometimes those friends save you from having to book a hotel.

Building relationships with people, helping each other out, sharing your resources—this is how you build a community. You should care enough to make your community better, to help people in your industry, to recognize and promote people when they deserve it.

Community building is probably the best thing I learned from the punk scene. We were surrounded by people who were interested in supporting their community, with a "rising tide lifts all ships" sort of attitude. But how does a scene like that get started? By people with a vested interest working together.

I live pretty far out in the boonies, which means that there weren't a lot of entertainment options growing up. I made the trip up to Pittsburgh, where there were what seemed like a thousand venues for shows, to see national touring acts only. Most of the time, my friends and I would go to the one official venue where local bands could play, which was supplemented by shows in basements and VFW halls, and the occasional high-school gym. We quickly learned how easily these few options could be taken away from us. If a band wrecked a place, that place would simply stop hosting shows. If kids left garbage all over the parking lot, no more shows. If too many people got drunk and rowdy, and a venue suffered from frequent visits from the police, you guessed it, no more shows. And if most of the attendees were sneaking in without paying, or if there were no crowd at all, then those venues could no longer afford to keep the doors open. The lesson was that if we didn't care about this community enough to be a real part of it, nobody else was going to care about keeping it going either. If your band wants to have a place to play, or if you want to have a space where you can listen to live music, then you need to support that scene.

We started seeing bands support each other by coming to shows that they weren't on the bill for. Often, regulars came out to a venue without even knowing who was playing that night. The crowd of regulars grew. People showed up on time for shows instead of just popping in for the headliner. Bands helped keep venues running by promoting them or lending a hand with basic functions like working the door. The punk club 924 Gilman had a rather famous rule: to play there, you also had to volunteer your time there.

"I used to work with my girlfriend Rayne on a zine called *Punk By The Slice*. It lasted for six months and six issues, and got tons of attention, most likely because it had the word "Punk" in the name. It was a submission-based zine and always consisted of an interview with a band, some reviews, some poems, some art, and a bunch of reviews of books or albums or something. It was a pretty standard punk zine. A lot of our friends helped work on it, and the zine always contained many different perspectives and points of view. It felt like we were making more than just a zine, but also a true outspoken punk community. We've never taken down the Facebook page for *Punk By The Slice*, and we still get records, cassettes, and tapes in the mail from time to time, even other zines. It is super exciting to get this stuff, and I always try to review it and print it in somebody else's zine or online or something, so the kind punks who sent it get something out of it. It's just weird being the person that gets stuff in the mail asking for reviews and recognition. We were just high-school kids when we made *Punk By The Slice*. However, being able to do a zine was the stepping stone for so many other projects since. I always say that being in the punk scene is like an "intro to everything" course. It's an intro to politics, philosophy, business, crafting, networking, etc. So that's the story of how I became part of the US-postal-service-based punk scene."

—Scott McMaster II, *Punk By The Slice*

This same sense of community can be cultivated by local businesses. The more I become involved in community events, the smaller Pittsburgh seems to be. There's so much collaboration between businesses. I see their support for each other's events as well as for their own physical community, and it's just as important to be an active part in that. If someone in your industry or your community is working on something you'd like to see thrive—a meetup, a collaborative project, or a co-working space—you should support it. Maybe you don't have much time to devote to others' ideas, but there are tiers of support, from just giving a project's signal a little boost via social media to showing up for events or volunteering your time to help make them happen.

East End Brewery strives to operate a zero-waste, environmentally sustainable brewery. So when it created its first "Pedal Pale Ale" kegs of the season, it teamed up with Bike Pittsburgh to deliver the beer in a suitably sustainable way. Together, they organized a bike ride. A few hundred people showed up to support the cause and spread the word about what it means to operate an environmentally sustainable business. They also helped haul kegs of beer to a mystery location for the ale's debut. Since Bike Pittsburgh cares about sustainability, and knows all the best bike routes in town, it was the perfect partner for this event. On top of raising awareness for something that both businesses care about, they also used the registration fees to raise funds to cover medical expenses for a friend at Agents of Change Recycling.

There are plenty of benefits to businesses' collaboration. As in the last example, you can help each other with things that may not be your area of expertise. East End Brewery had an idea for an event, but maybe needed some help with the logistics of setting up a bike ride. Bike Pittsburgh provided that knowledge and experience. Also, partnering up expands your potential reach. Business A has its set of fans, and Business B has its own. When they support each other's events, they're increasing the pool of people who might also support that event. Local businesses stand to benefit a lot from the successes of other local businesses. When people buy shirts from me, they're helping me out. I'm making money, so I get to keep being a business. But their purchases also mean that I'm able to pay a local screen-printing company to produce those shirts. More work means that the company is able to keep the place running, which means I'm able to keep getting shirts and posters produced. Since the screen-printing company also hosts meetups for people in my industry, I have yet another vested interest in helping it.

Much like when you buy a record, you're supporting not only their efforts but the efforts of their label and the studio where that record was produced. When you support a local business that supports *other* local businesses, that sense of community gets stronger. And when a town has a supportive environment, it affords its businesses a chance to grow and expand. Which means you, as a community member, have a wider variety of offerings to choose from. Local businesses can sustain town centers, connect people through economic and social relationships, and contribute to local causes. By supporting your local economy, you also support all those efforts.

"We found that, in our area, the local scene was desperate for a home. We set out to create that for kids in the under-twenty-one scene by opening Club Octane. It was an old warehouse storefront in the outskirts of Pittsburgh. It wasn't the most ideal location or even the most ideal building, but we were hoping we could overcome that, and we did. We held shows almost every weekend for about three years in little old Charleroi, Pennsylvania. We held CD-release parties for local bands who were trying so hard to make it, and made it easy for local kids to come see national bands.

We made it possible for local kids to come to shows without having to drive to 'the city.' I can't tell you how many times I have heard from kids who say 'I grew up coming to Octane' or 'I was there *every* weekend.' Those are the reasons why we did what we did.

I ate, slept, and breathed the local scene until I had my first daughter. I can remember one time, when Terror was set to play at Octane, everyone kept warning me about the destruction that was going to happen to the club that night and how they are so well-known for 'crowd surfing' (one of the few things I had rules against inside). I remember going down there, baby on hip, to talk to them about my NO-crowd-surfing rule because I didn't want any kids getting hurt (our average age of patrons was around fifteen), and they were the most understanding and amazing guys about it." —Evie Bagwell, Club Octane

Another thing we started to see in the community was fans who called out destructive behavior when they saw it. Sneaking in through the back earned you glares instead of high fives from your friends, and leaving litter would get you at least a *hey, that's not cool*. Calling out people for hurting your industry isn't as easy or as fun as promoting the good stuff, but it's just as necessary.

One day, Dan Cassaro, designer extraordinaire, received an email from Showtime, the television network. For those of you not entrenched in design, a big problem in the industry is what's called spec work: work that's done on speculation—i.e. if the prospective client likes it and decides to use it, then you get paid for it. Otherwise, you get nothing. For those of you familiar with the music business, it's as shady as the famous "pay to play" model. There's never a contract to protect your work, and sometimes, even if a client does decide to use the work, the compensation is in "exposure" (meaning she tells everybody about that excellent *free* work she got from you). Many designers refuse to work on spec, but some contests can tempt fledgling designers with promises of being "good for your portfolio," that it will help you "gain recognition." It's often harder for newer designers to say no, so companies keep doing it. The most egregious offenses are those that come from companies that have more than enough profits to compensate others fairly for their work. Enter Showtime.

"Hi Dan,
We're reaching out on behalf of Showtime, because we're looking for artists with an eclectic style to create a piece focused on the upcoming fight Mayweather/ Maidana 2: Mayhem. In May, Marcos 'El Chino' Maidana gave Floyd 'Money' Mayweather his most competitive fight in years. Mayweather pulled out a majority decision victory in an exciting fight that many thought was even closer than the judges scored it. They [*sic*] are set to meet again on September 13, in a highly anticipated rematch. We want to capture the intensity of the fight, and what better way to do so than through art!

We explored your work, and we're digging your style. We think you could bring a unique perspective to the competition! The winner will be flown to Vegas, where their artwork will be featured at the MGM Grand and in Showtime events and broadcasts throughout the week. Submissions are due by 8/26, and the top ten will be voted on by the SHOSports community on social media. For all the contest info, check out the website. What do you think? Let us know if you have any Qs and feel free to share with your peers! Thanks!"

Showtime specifically approached an established designer, who has done paid work for clients like Nike, VH1, and Lands' End, to see if he'd spend his time working on artwork that *might* be featured in events surrounding the fight—from which they will be pulling in mountains of cash—for no pay.

This is Dan's response.

"Thanks for thinking of me for this! Glad you are digging my style! It is with great sadness that I must decline your enticing offer to work for you for free. I know that boxing matches in Las Vegas are extremely low-budget affairs, especially ones with nobodies like Floyd 'Money' Mayweather. I heard he pulled in only 80 million for his last fight! I also understand that a 'mom and pop' cable channel like Showtime must rely on handouts just to keep the lights on these days. Thanks a lot, Obama! My only hope is that you can scrape up a few dollars from this grassroots event at the MGM Grand to put yourself back in the black. If that happens, you might consider using some of that money to compensate people to do the thing they are professionally trained to do. Godspeed, Dan."

It's snarky, and funny, and people in Dan's industry can surely relate to such offers to work for free. But why bother to write this response, let alone publish it, instead of simply saying no or ignoring the request altogether? As someone who wants to continue working in design, Dan cares about his industry's welfare. He explained to *Adweek*, "I wanted to let people know that while it's good to say no to this kind of work, it's even better to explain to everyone why this business model is unacceptable." Aside from blowing off some steam generated by these kinds of crowdsourcing campaigns, he's also helped to educate people about why this practice is bad for the industry. He's calling out terrible behavior that hurts his community.

Your community doesn't necessarily have to be a physical one. While I'm big on supporting local business, my industry is a global one. There are people all over the world who care about the same things you do, who share your ideals. You can find those people at festivals and conferences, or you can find them in scene reports in zines, or on this crazy new thing called the Internet. Being able to connect in that way makes it easier than ever to find like-minded people to collaborate with, as well as people with different opinions to learn from. You can work with these people by using whatever skills that you have to make your community better. Bands have put on benefit shows for any number of causes, from food drives for their community to paying for medical care for one of their regulars or just raising awareness for a cause. Artists sell their work to benefit causes that they care about or donate their time and talents to charities. Jello Biafra from the Dead Kennedys even ran for mayor of San Francisco. That's a real thing that happened. You use what you know, and you work together with people to fill in the blanks. The world, or at least small sections of it, has been changed by lesser things than a punk band or an art project.

When you're sincere, you care about a thing, and you pour your heart into it, good things come from it. I know it sounds all unicorns-and-rainbows, but I've found it to be true. Conan O'Brien's "work hard and be kind" statement is actually really solid advice. You don't want to work with a pain in the ass unless you really, really have to. You get work somehow—word of mouth, an advertisement, Google-fu—but you keep work because you're good, you're easy to get along with, and you deliver work on time. Two out of three will do, and, arguably, being pleasant to work with may be the biggest deciding factor. Getting involved in projects that I care about has been a huge factor in connecting with people and getting work.

When people in your community are doing something good that you feel is important, support that. When they're doing something that hurts your community, call it out. You have a responsibility to your community to consider the impact that your employees, your projects, your client choices have. Stand for something.

People can be squeamish when it comes to promotion. It's easy to equate advertising with the sleazy ad exec who persuades people to buy things they don't need. Using shady practices and trumped-up statistics is something that you can avoid, but promoting yourself isn't. Whether you have a service-based business or a product-based one, you're going to have to tell people what you're doing. It's a lovely thought: once you make this amazing product that everyone's going to want, people will find you and bang down the door to hand you their cash. In real life (where your rent is due) you'll need to spend a good chunk of your time pitching your business.

There's a lot to be learned from musicians when it comes to promoting, because bands live or die by it. Musicians need you to know that they have released a new album, so that you can buy it. If you don't hear their new music, you might not be inclined to come out and see them on tour, which is funded in part by those album sales. And if you don't come see them live, they would lose not only the take from the door that night but an opportunity to strengthen and grow their fan base, which puts them right back at cold-selling the next album.

This is not a complicated concept, and you can likely see how it applies to your own business. If I'm trying to get people to hire me to make ceramic mugs for them, of course I want to have a shop full of examples of work that I've done, and plenty of happy customers [read *fans*] to vouch for my work and to buy things again in the future. But the first step is making people aware that I make ceramic mugs. To build that awareness means saying it, out loud, a lot.

Bands are great at this, because when they have a show, they just won't shut up about it. Don't act like you didn't know that a show was coming up, because they've mentioned it four times just this week. A touring band will happily tell you when they're in your town next, who they're playing with, and where exactly you can find out more information about them. People who aren't used to this sort of promotion, on the other hand, feel really uncomfortable about it. Maybe they feel like they're bothering people, or they don't want to seem *salesy*. There are lists of rules for how not to promote yourself on various social-media channels.

The truth is that people are bombarded with noise, especially on the Internet. They're overloaded with information all day, every day. So posting that starting this fall, you'll be offering custom knitted hats at the new store you're opening isn't enough. Even when dealing with people who are interested in what you do, it's your job to remind them that you exist, and that you are still making those adorable hats that they like so much. It takes several impressions before your brain even absorbs the information, and sometimes several more before you're inclined to act on it. I'll frequently skip over five or six of my friends' postings of the same article before I finally read it—and these are people whose opinions and thoughts I already value. It's even more difficult to get attention from strangers. While it probably seems to you like this new business is all you ever talk about, you may be surprised to find out how many people have missed that information. I've been doing wedding photography since 2007, and I still have relatives who are unaware that I offer that service.

Promote yourself, but also promote your friends. When your friends do something cool, tell everybody. Announce interesting things going on in your community or in your industry. If your business makes custom skate decks, become a resource for things going on in your community, like an event at a new skate park or a learn-to-skate program. Don't do it because your community may return the favor later (although, often, they tend to), but because if you can't get excited about your friends doing cool shit, then what the hell's the point? And if you aren't interested in what's going on in your industry, then maybe you've chosen the wrong industry.

So you're getting comfortable with the idea of talking about your business. You're posting things to social media, you're writing blogs, you've told your great aunt Cathy and her quilting circle about your hand-made artisan quilting hoops. Everyone in your circle knows about your new venture, but your circle is still small. How do you find new people? What a lot of promoting comes down to is figuring out whose audience would also appreciate your work.

Generally speaking, concerts are made up of bands that have some kind of common thread. If people are fans of one band, there's a good chance that they'll also enjoy the other bands on the bill, which creates an opportunity for all the bands to find new fans (and for fans to find new music). One of the best ways that I found new music as a kid was through splits and compilation albums. Splits are just what they sound like—two bands split a record. One benefit is that bands are sharing the expense of having the record produced, but the other benefit is that it allows both bands to reach a new audience. Signals Midwest and Worship This! put out a split, on which they went one step further and covered each other's songs. Signals Midwest fans will buy it and hear Worship This! and vice versa. Considering the bands play shows together fairly often, there's a good chance that fans of one band will enjoy the other. And with cover songs, fans have an opportunity to hear a song they already like in a new style (or a style they're familiar with on a new song). As another example, Anti-Flag put out a series they called *20 Years of Hell*, which was a set of 7" records. Because Anti-Flag are a well-established band, they don't really need to worry about having another name on the album to help sell it, and they could have easily just put out the box set and collected their money. Instead, they chose a different band for the B-side of each record—again, selecting bands you might enjoy if you are already a fan of Anti-Flag. They saw an opportunity to get bands that they liked and respected in front of a larger audience.

Compilations are more along the lines of a mixtape. Record labels produced most of the compilations we picked up, so they'd include a bunch of bands that are on their label (which tend to have a common thread). Some, though, are put together with different criteria. One of my favorite compilations, *Short Music for Short People*, featured thirty-second (or shorter) songs, written specifically for the project, from 101 bands. For the price of a CD, you get to hear 101 different bands. David Hayes also put together a compilation album—*The Thing That Ate Floyd*—that's effectively just bands he likes. The idea, however, is the same. Someone curates the tracks that will be included, and if you're generally a fan of the same type of music as that curator, you'll likely find some new bands to listen to.

This is great for bands, but how does this apply to you and your business? I'm a designer, and designers don't make records. But designers do make collaborative projects that work in the same way. Dan Cassaro started a 50/50 project, in which he asked fifty artists to illustrate each state's motto. Nate Utesch's zine, *Ferocious Quarterly*, includes artists and writers. Artists who have an existing audience ask for other collaborators, and they put those people in front of their audience. They think these people are pretty cool and hope you will too. There are many opportunities to collaborate with other businesses, which benefit both parties, just like split albums. Guest blogs are used in nearly every industry to the same effect—the owner of the blog gets a day off from creating content, and the guest blogger benefits from that blogger's existing fan base.

Interesting work results from unexpected partnerships. While people don't generally put musicians and comedians into the same category, they both create audio. Jonah Ray, co-host of *The Meltdown* on Comedy Central, started something called The Mutual Appreciation Society. As part of his effort to treat his comedy like a band, he put out a 7" album. This is a thing he could have done entirely on his own—written the material, recorded an album, and promoted it in the usual ways. Instead, he took the opportunity to pair comedians with musicians, considering either pre-existing relationships or simply things that he thought would go well together. Each 7" has comedy on one side, music on the other.

Sometimes the connections are obvious, but sometimes you find some really weird—and really interesting—cross-promotion opportunities. This was something that happened out of necessity for our tiny scene, because I live in the middle of nowhere, and there simply weren't that many bands. My husband played in a punk band when I met him, but some of his friends played in a metal band. Some of his friends played in a funny pop-punk band, and some were in a political crusty band, and some played grindcore, and some played rap-funk. And they frequently played shows that were some combination of those styles, because there weren't enough bands of any one type to create a cohesive bill. Maybe the common thread in their music wasn't clear. No one would look at those bands objectively and think, *this show will be successful.* But there was no mass exodus at the end of a set and no clean lines between fan bases. The common thread in the music may not have been obvious, but it was there, and we quickly found that fans of the political band really liked the rap-funk. It wasn't a conscious decision that the bands had made, to widen their fanbase. It was just people that make cool shit, getting together. And it worked.

Historically, mixing genres in that way has been met with more resistance. In some scenes, trying to get the metalheads in the same venue as the punk kids resulted in violence. But there's a definite fast and loud correlation between the two, and eventually they started integrating. DRI opened for Slayer, Metallica covered some Misfits songs, and I somehow found myself at a show that put The Offspring and Cypress Hill on a bill together. Collaborate with people who do similar work to yours, but consider collaborations with people whose projects are different. It's a great opportunity to meet people whom you have more in common with than you might have thought.

Many punk bands found another area that had a fast and loud correlation—skate and surf videos. It seems like an obvious connection now, because those cultures tend to be very ingrained, but it wasn't always that way. At some point, a producer or a director or a kid with a camera realized that extreme sports needed an aggressive soundtrack, and they found it in punk. All of a sudden, those bands had a whole new audience. Kids in

Kansas who may not have had any exposure to the punk scene would buy a skate video and hear NOFX. Many of my friends first heard Pennywise on *Tony Hawk's Pro Skater*, a popular skateboarding video-game series. From that exposure, bands got to tour places like Australia or Japan; places that had a surf or skate culture now had a punk culture, too.

Embracing this concept was a huge help to my photography business, which is mostly brides and bands. I shoot a lot of weddings, and I shoot a lot of live music and promotional portraits. I used to keep those completely separate in my marketing, because I thought that one group really wasn't going to care about the other. There wasn't an obvious connection to me between those two sets of people. Of course, just because there isn't an obvious connection doesn't mean there isn't a connection. It turned out that a lot of the couples that I booked were really into music, specifically the sort of music that I tended to cover. When you're looking at strangers on the Internet, common ground can be a deciding factor in whether you're going to meet up or hire them. When a couple that thinks I might judge them for playing Slayer at their reception sees that I was photographing Hatebreed the week before, they're suddenly a lot more comfortable around me. Bands, however, didn't seem to care that I was shooting weddings, but the fact that I did other styles of photography didn't deter them from hiring me. They were also more likely to refer me to their friends who were getting married. Because I allowed for the possibility that those two worlds might have a little overlap in their Venn diagram, I have a larger audience.

The nature of distribution, the rules for getting your work out there, is changing for creative people of all kinds, which can sound really intimidating. It's like the Wild West out there. Marketing tactics that people have relied on for decades aren't working anymore. Those old rules for how you were allowed to show your work to the world are crumbling, and there are no new rules. Scary stuff. But also, it's liberating stuff, because now you

"The biggest thing I've noticed after coming back into the music scene three years ago is that shows are almost irrelevant. When I was younger and Skies Bleed Black was getting started, everything revolved around the concert. Youth made us hungry. We would plan shows months or years in advance. Flyers were made, photocopied illegally at our parents' work, and plastered everywhere. Practices were of the utmost importance. The small shows were just as important as the larger ones. Technology has made us lazy. Now, we make our Facebook event, spam our friends online, and see if anyone takes the bait. Getting a show booked or getting people to come out was never easy. It still isn't. It might be harder now than it ever was. With so many ways to reach people now, it has made it easier for people to block it all out.

We had no social networks to promote ourselves when we started. No booking agents, no managers, no promotion companies or record labels to get us gigs. You had to have an "in" or work really hard for one. A concert was one of the only ways to get your band started. Today, you and your friends can get on a computer; record in Garageband; and come up with a demo in a day; upload it to Facebook, YouTube, Myspace, Bandcamp, or Reverbnation; and promote it before mom gets done baking the band cookies.

Shows were the building blocks of every band. Technology changed that. Everything a band does now revolves around the social network. As it should. That's where the times have taken us. A good social network is probably your best way to build fans now. For us, the show was our social network. It was our home. It's where we made fans, friends, and connections. It's where our bands built our culture. Something you can't build with just an online presence. People got to know our band through dank clubs, clouds of smoke, stained floors, and burned-out light bulbs. They could heckle us. They could fight us. They could hang with us. I owe a lot to websites like Myspace, but all our "Friends" could never replace the kid jumping on stage to grab a mic." —David Wilson, Skies Bleed Black, Dog Days get to make those rules up. Since no one's done it before, no one's made up rules to stop anyone from doing it again. It's probably never been easier to put your work out there, on a platform where anyone can see it, thanks to the magic of the Internet. Whatever gatekeepers existed to keep your work out of their magazines, their TV shows, or their radio stations can't stop you from putting whatever it is that you do online. For something like $90 a year, I can set up my own website and put absolutely anything that I want on it. Anything. And if that $90 a year is too great a barrier, you can set up a blog to do the very same thing for free. I used a free Wordpress blog as my website for a really long time when I started out. You can make something, and you can make it immediately available to people if you so choose.

The flip side is that everyone is doing just that. So how do you get any attention for the thing that you're doing over the things that others are doing? There are a ton of books about marketing that get into this aspect of business—you can be first, you can be unique, you can cater to a smaller niche, or you can just spin your story better than everyone else. You can go for shock value—Negative Trend plastered a town with flyers featuring Hitler and proceeded to get banned from every venue in the city before they played a single show. That may not be the sort of reaction you're after, but they certainly got a lot of publicity. Whatever your method, it's important to figure out what's unique about your work, so that you can tell other people about it. Negative Trend seemed to be going for Most Offensive Band. But maybe your auto-detailing shop specializes in VW Bugs. Or your catering business uses produce from a garden that you grow yourself. Or your cleaning service will leave a mint on clients' pillows and fresh flowers on the table. Figure out what makes your business, which maybe a jillion other people are also doing, different. Yes, this is going to take more time and effort than just putting out your virtual shingle and hoping that customers show up. The downside to there being endless opportunity for promotion is that you have to fight a lot harder for attention.

Adapt or die. There are a lot of sentiments I'm sort of tired of hearing, like *kids these days with their giving clients digital photos instead of prints* and *we used to make all our money off prints, you know*. You used to. Now you don't. What do you plan to do now? And don't say *cry about it*. Crying about it is not a viable business model. Maybe you raise your prices for those digital negatives, or maybe you make a compelling argument for getting those prints made. What you can't do is complain that you can no longer do business in the exact same way that you used to. It's not productive. The good thing about the changing landscape of business is that you can adapt however you want. You don't have to wait for someone to give you a job or for a client to hire you in order to start making something that you think is good. You don't have to use the same pricing structure as anyone else. You don't have to make a physical product if you think a digital one serves your clients better, and you don't need permission to put your work out there. People willing to be clever, to figure out how to do more with less, to work around obstacles, will do okay.

Commonwealth Press auctioned off a brick. You may have deduced from the "Press" in the name that they do not make bricks. In fact, they are screenprinters. But one day, they walked into their storefront to find that someone had thrown a brick through the window. This was a giant bummer. They had to clean up that mess and replace the window, and probably all before they'd had their morning coffee. Not to mention, they still had to open the shop that day. Instead of despairing, they decided to auction off the brick to raise funds to replace the window. They threw in a free t-shirt and some stickers, which they wrapped around the brick. And then they made a simple post on Facebook, explaining what had happened, asking people to make their bids in the comments. It became A Thing.

Other businesses donated goods or gift certificates to be raffled off with the brick. The bids went up. Commonwealth added in some tickets to their upcoming Beer Barge event, and bids went up some more. Local news stations came in to interview the owners, and by the end of it, Commonwealth raised far more cash than they needed to replace the window, so they gave the excess to charity. At a time when it seems like everyone is trying to sell you something, how did this get noticed over every other post?

It's a good story. They took something negative and turned it into something really positive that didn't benefit only them but their community as well.

It's a weird story. *Commonwealth Press auctioned a brick for HOW MUCH?*

Part of the reason that other business owners offered to help is that Commonwealth Press are involved in their community. They support other local businesses, and those same businesses wanted to support them. And while they could have just kept the extra cash after fixing the window, they put that money back into the community instead. It's downright heartwarming.

This particular approach is not something you're going to find in a book on how to market your business, and it's not likely a result that you can replicate for yourself. The point is to find a strategy that is specific to you. In what ways can you be clever about your promotions? How can you create something positive in your own community? Most of the time, these aren't calculated moves. Commonwealth just wanted to fix their window. Often, just putting in the time to be involved and trying to do good things gets you noticed.

On the other hand, clever ways to market your work can be very calculated. Before Nathan Martin was heading up Deeplocal, he worked with an anarchist group called Carbon Defense League (and before that, a touring punk band). When he taught a graduate class I took, he was the sort of professor who would give you extra credit for garnering a cease-and-desist letter (excellent press). Most of the league's work involved hacking existing structures. In one project, the league reverse-engineered the Nintendo Gameboy by hacking the game cartridge and uploading their own game, called Super Kid Fighter, which allowed kids to produce content. But how do you get it to kids? After they had uploaded their own program, they simply returned it to the store, to be resold to someone else. Kids got to play the game they created, and parents and retailers ended up talking about it. CDL later spoke and held hacker conferences, like Madhack Conference in Barcelona. While this approach is sort of illegal, it also ends with their projects making the news.

Again, these folks have all figured out what makes their business different, unique, interesting. They've adopted marketing techniques that wouldn't work for just anybody, and certainly don't fall under your usual "10 ways to get people to notice your business" style of advice. But in addition to staying true to the individual ways that their businesses run, Commonwealth Press and CDL have also both gotten the word out in a way that matters to them. Commonwealth Press honestly cares about their community. Carbon Defense League really believed in teaching kids that they could be content creators, not just consumers. Neither of these efforts were solely concocted to get press, but because they chose something authentic to them, they were able to tell an interesting story, and they got a ton of attention anyway.

MAKE

I'm always working on something. Most times, I'm working on several somethings, split between client work and personal projects. I've found that the more work you put out there, the better the chances that something will stick with the right person. It's important to show people what you've done, but it's just as important to show them what you're doing.

One thing I picked up from the punk scene is the idea of being prolific, although that's probably not the word they'd use. Friends weren't in just one band, they were in several. They were rarely ever working on only one project, and not all of those projects were necessarily original music—some friends ran venues or labels. They'd collaborate, doing backing vocals for another band's album or filling in on guitar for a show. There's a fun game we like to play with backing vocals on early 90s tracks called *Is That Davey Havok?* Perhaps an even better example is Mikey Erg, who is likely starting a new band or joining an existing one this very second.

I know, there's only so much time in a day, and you'd like to fill some of that with eating or sleeping or quality time with loved ones. You can't do every single cool project that occurs to you, and deciding where to spend your time is an important part of running a business. But when you are thoughtful about the projects you take on and the work you choose to do, you may be surprised by how much time you are able to find to do the work.

One of the benefits to producing a lot of work is practice. If you're playing guitar for four different bands, you're getting a lot of practice time on that instrument. And when you work on personal projects that aren't necessarily for any particular client, you have a lot of room for experimentation. When I just draw whatever I like, I get to try different styles and techniques that I might not otherwise have time to mess around with. Some of my attempts turn out terribly (occasionally experiments fail), and sometimes they end up being another trick that I add to my repertoire. Because I produce a lot of work and spend so much time with it, I get to try a lot of things. Doing the work is the only real way to find your own style.

Of course, there is something to be said for focusing on one project, although being focused and being prolific aren't mutually exclusive. Bands have been plenty successful without dabbling in side projects, and have put just as much work out there. According to Mr. Rogers, "deep and simple is far more essential than shallow and complex." Mr. Rogers seems to favor specialization (deep and simple) over the idea of being a jack-of-all-trades (shallow and complex). Whether your approach is to put all your efforts into one project or to spread your efforts across many ideas, the advice is the same—make (or do, for you service-industry types). Whatever it is you want to create a business from, do a lot of it. The "10,000 hours of practice to make an expert" theory is widespread, and there's a similar one in photography circles about your first 10,000 photos being terrible, and it's as good an arbitrary number as any. Often, the hardest part of a project is just getting it started, making something you can build on. You can edit a bad page, but not a blank one. Just make your terrible thing, and go from there.

All this production gives you the opportunity to steal another practice from musicians—iterating. Bands will write a few songs to practice, then play a show and see how they do. They're iterating in the wild, with live feedback. You can do the same thing.

Say you're trying to start a personal-training service. You're going to do your research, figure out a plan for a workout, and then try it out with your client. You can look at what worked and what didn't, and make changes to improve your time together for the next session. This last part, the analysis and editing, isn't an opportunity that you get until you put your work out there. Shipping is hard, and stressful, and it's much easier to just hold on to your project. Keep researching. Tweak that plan. Redesign that flyer one more time. At this point, you're procrastiworking. Some people call it "sharpening pencils." You're doing things that seem like work but are ultimately just ways to stall on doing the actual work. And as Amy Poehler says, talking about the thing isn't the thing—doing the thing is the thing. You need to just go out and do it.

Now, the moral of the story isn't *just go do things and be terrible at them and it'll work itself out probably*, because that's terrible advice. Research and planning are wonderful, essential things that you absolutely should be doing before you up and start a business. But at some point, you'll need to recognize that you've done enough, that you've reached the point of diminishing returns on your research, and that this thing is as organized as it's going to get. The idea is not to let the fear of failing, or not being exactly perfect, keep you from ever doing anything. Things will go wrong, no matter how much you plan, and you will find areas that need to be improved. You'll improve those things, you'll try again, and you'll find even more ways to make what you're doing better. And every time you put something out there and survive, it gets less scary to put work out there.

Part of the reason people are hesitant to experiment is that they worry a project won't turn out like they'd hoped. However, you don't necessarily have to publicize all your work. The very point of experimenting is to try new, different things that may not work out. The best thing to take the pressure off yourself is to remember that if whatever you create here is terrible, nobody ever has to know about it. I know, people share everything they do on the Internet the instant it happens. But making and sharing can be entirely separate endeavors, and it's important to be thoughtful about which projects you put out there. You certainly want to promote the work that you're doing and show it to the world, but make sure that you're showing the kind of work that you want to *do*. People will hire you for the kind of work they see you doing.

In his talk "Betray the Institution," Brandon Rike uses the metaphor of a brick wall. When you're building a red-brick wall, you want people to give you red bricks. People will offer you rocks or blue squares. You could try to cobble those things into your brick wall, even though they don't really fit so well. Or you can choose to pass on them, and wait for that red brick that you really need. The idea is to make sure that the work you're doing (and, more importantly, the work you're showing and promoting) is going to get you where you want to go.

We had a local metal band, let's call them Name Withheld. What they really wanted to do was write and play metal songs, but what they spent most of their time doing was playing covers of southern-rock songs at bars. Because they're decent musicians, it's not that hard to knock out a cover of Brown Eyed Girl, and when a friend offered them a paying gig at a local bar, they took it. People saw them there, and offered them similar gigs, and they took those, too. They ended up spending most of their time practicing for and playing these shows, and had little time left to spend on what they actually wanted to do.

I've seen this same thing happen with a lot of photographer friends. Once, a friend was bemoaning the fact that she spends most of her time doing family portraits and newborn photos. When I went to her website, it was filled with sessions for families and newborns. Her instagram feed was all smiling babies. She'd made a habit of blogging every session that she shot, regardless of the type, and when people started seeing more family stuff, they started booking her for more family stuff, and the cycle continued. How could anyone who came across her site possibly know that she hates shooting family and newborn portraits, and really wants to book jobs for advertising? Try to be objective when you look at your website or social-media accounts. What are you telling the world that you do? What do you really want to be doing?

Early on, when I didn't have many clients to carve out time for, taking on projects seemed like a very simple decision. There wasn't much else taking up my time, so I worked on whatever was offered to me. Later, I started working full-time at a day job, and my business started really taking off. A lot of you may be in the same boat: you're working full-time all day and then working on your business when you get home at night. At this point, you have to be more careful about how you spend your time. When you're working 40 or more hours a week at one job, on top of your other social and familial responsibilities, it can feel impossible to find the time to do any more work. You need to be very self-aware, and frequently adjust your schedule. Balancing your work with the rest of your life can get tricky with freelancing, and it's likely a thing you'll continue to struggle with. Collaborators become friends, and you love your work, so it's also sort of your hobby, and everything becomes an amorphous blob. But your time can be about work without being work. A professor introduced me to the "bed, bath, and bus" theory—that you come up with your best ideas when your brain is autopiloting your body through mundane tasks (going to bed, bathing, sitting on the bus, or driving). Time spent not working can be great for your business, as well as for all those other relationships in your life that you want to thrive.

When I started freelancing, money wasn't as much a consideration in terms of how I spent my time, since no one was paying me any. I had only a few clients, so it left me with a lot of free time to work on my own projects. Then, my trade-off was between working on a poster series and watching a *House* marathon on USA, which is a pretty easy choice. The busier you get, and the more clients you're juggling, the more carefully you'll need to weigh how you spend your time.

I made a lot of excuses for why I wasn't furthering my business: *I couldn't possibly, I have a day job, no one's hiring me for that, I'm too busy, I'm tired, it's a full moon tonight, I can't spend any time on marketing when I have client work to do, I don't have time.* Eventually, I realized the things that I said were holding me back were things that I actually had control over. Ditching those excuses and taking responsibility for how I spent my time allowed me to do the kind of work I wanted. But being honest about those excuses was also harsh. Excuses can be warm, cozy things, and they made me feel justified in my behavior. *I don't have time* was a common phrase that I found coming out of my mouth, until I realized that getting what I wanted meant that I'd have to look at the choices I had made. It's easier for me to say *I don't have time* than to admit that I was choosing to spend my time on things that weren't very important to me or that I was being unrealistic with the amount of work I was accepting. I get the same 24 hours that anybody else gets (yes, even Beyoncé). How I spend those hours is up to me. I was still trying to do every job that came my way, and sometimes my business was stretched in too many directions. Then I'd get burned out on work and spend too much time vegged out on the couch, until I was overcome with guilt for not doing the work, and the cycle would start over. I was managing my time poorly.

One concept that helped me make better decisions about my time was learning to look at the opportunity cost of doing things. Economically speaking, it's a more complex concept than what I'm presenting here, but at the basic level, opportunity cost is what you're giving up to get this other thing when you can't do both—and you can spend your time only once. When it comes to actual monetary cost, these decisions seem so much easier, but I wasn't really considering my time. Your time is a valuable resource that you need to learn to protect.

Looking at how I'm spending my time as an active choice, instead of as a thing that's happening to me, forces me to make better decisions. Not to mention, I get to feel better about those decisions. When I was taking on every job I could, struggling to fit everything in, I became resentful about the amount of work I was doing. I was trading sleep for those extra work hours (your health, by the way, is another valuable resource to protect). The burnout struggle is real, especially in the early days of getting your business off the ground. So I started to spend more time considering what doing each job would cost me.

Generally speaking, your opportunity cost for business ventures will be some combination of time and money. I can't possibly do every project that comes my way or pops into my brain, so I have to consider the opportunity cost of doing each one. If I choose to spend an hour on a personal project, that's an hour I'm not spending on paid client work. I'm giving up the money I could have made there. When I'm shooting a festival out of state, I'm giving up those hours that I could be working, I'm giving up some cash for gas and food. If I spend all of my time playing southern rock at dive bars, then I don't have my Saturdays free to play metal clubs. There's always a trade-off.

In a lot of cases, that opportunity cost is all that's stopping you. I've heard people say *I'd love to do gig posters* or *I really want to start a t-shirt line*, and I've said those sorts of things myself. It's easy to think that you need a client to hire you in order to do that work. Really, you don't have to wait around for someone to hire you to make a poster or a t-shirt. You're free to create your own personal projects, to make something just because *you* had the idea to do it. Designer Winston Smith used to make posters for bands that didn't exist. You know how sometimes you'll say a weird phrase and think *that'd be a good name for a band*? He went ahead and made flyers for those imaginary bands. The flyer would just read "Friday" with an address that didn't exist. If you have an idea that you want to spend your time on, you don't need anyone's permission to do it. You just need to weigh the cost.

Money and time aren't your only considerations, though. Sometimes, opportunity cost comes in social standing, which can be a major roadblock to people's true passions. The trade might be that if I do this art exhibit, my friends will think I'm weird. Or my parents will change the subject when people ask them what I do. It could be that if I quit the family business, our Thanksgiving dinners are going to be awkward. Maybe my friends will complain that I'm never available to go out at night because I'm working. There's always a trade-off. It's important that you be aware of what your business pursuits cost you, because they're costing you. You're the one that will have to make and live with those decisions, so you need to make sure that pursuit is worth it to you. People will have all sorts of comments and opinions about what you're doing, but they aren't the ones who have to commit to it. You do. And these trade-offs can be much easier to handle if they're something you go into with open eyes, something you consciously agree to. It's the difference between feeling buried under work and making a plan in which you feel good about the work you're doing. Take some time to consider what you'll need to give up to make this venture successful and whether you're okay with it. And when your reflex reaction to an opportunity is *I don't have time*, take a second look at what you'd have to give up to make the time. Sometimes it's worth it, sometimes it's not. But now, it's a choice that you've consciously made, instead of defaulting to whatever you'd been spending your time doing.

I like to make time for personal projects, because I've had a lot of great opportunities come out of personal work. This is a concept that's probably more familiar to artist and maker types than service-industry types, but it's just working on something that's self-initiated instead of something that a client has hired you to do. As an example, I started a poster series based on *Firefly*, a culty, canceled space-western TV show that you should watch immediately. I thought it would be fun to do a poster for each episode, since there are only fourteen of them, and I wanted to do the posters in a sort of retro sci-fi style. I thought it would be fun, so I carved out time to work on them around other projects. As such, I've finished seven posters over four years. Originally, I didn't have any intention of this being a money-making endeavor, but once I started putting them out there, people started asking where they could buy them. Now I've turned a little fun project into something that makes me a bit of extra cash every month. And aside from the direct sales, I've also had people who liked that style commission work from me. So just showing that I can do a different style of illustration also resulted in extra work. It's still not getting priority over client work, but it's something that's worth it to me to carve out a bit of time for every month.

I've also had some great opportunities come out of other, technically sort-of-failed projects. However, these things mostly came much later, when I was working on something else—and I'm always working on something.

A friend who was throwing a music festival in London got in touch with me about doing a poster to advertise the event. I did a hand-lettered poster for it, and one of the featured bands was Bobby Joe Ebola & the Children Macnuggits. I sent it off, and then I found some other work to do.

Six or eight months later, I was going down to Baltimore to photograph Insubordination Fest, where Bobby Joe Ebola were playing. I shot their set, and I met the guys after to shake their hands and say that I liked their music. We talked a bit, the festival came up, and I mentioned that if they ever needed any artwork done, to look me up. I sent them the photos when I got home, and again found some other work to do.

Maybe another five months later, Corbett, vocalist for Bobby Joe Ebola, got in touch with me about doing a book cover. They were going to put out the *Bobby Joe Ebola Songbook*, with lyrics and chords, fun illustrations, stories about touring, and other ephemera. They were meeting with the publisher, they needed a book cover, and they needed it in about three days. He said, "can you draw me a rabbit smoking a cigarette?" and I did. I sent over sketches, and after some back and forth, we landed on a cover that he was really into. But for whatever reason, they went with someone else to do the cover and art-direct the interior stuff, which Corbett was very apologetic about. I told him that it's business and no hard feelings, and that I hoped the band sold a million copies. Which I wholeheartedly meant, because he's good people. Once again, I found some other work to fill my time with.

A few months later (which puts us at close to a year and half since the start of this story), Corbett emailed me again. Even though the cover didn't work out, the band wanted me to contribute some interior illustrations, and I said I'd love to. That's how I went from doing a poster for a festival in London to having some of my work in the same book as

Winston Smith and Jason Chandler and Mitch Clem. You really never know who's going to see your work or where you might end up as a result.

Booking that gig was pretty off-chance, and it took a lot of patience, but it's not the only "how did you land that?" story of mine that goes that way. I learned from the bands that were making things happen that it took a lot of work to make those things happen. There are a lot of false starts, as well as opportunities or connections that don't materialize until years after the fact. When you see just the end result, you think *oh, they're so lucky*. But if you look behind the scenes of most overnight-success stories, you can see that they have been putting in the work for years. The bands that are doing well for themselves are the ones that just keep making new work, putting it out there, and trying new things. Slowly and steadily building your business is a lot less glamorous than getting discovered and thrust into the spotlight, but it's generally a lot more successful.

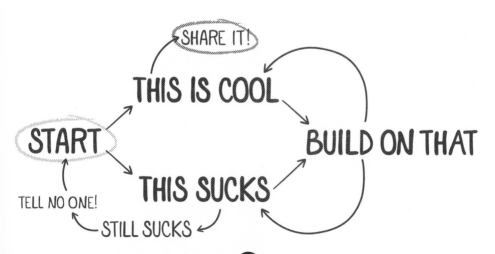

WHO THE HELL ARE THE RAMONES?

For a lot of new small businesses, it can feel like the biggest struggle is just getting your name out there. The Internet may have decreased the barriers in some ways (the only thing stopping you from setting up social-media accounts for your business is a few minutes of free time), but it also means there's a lot more noise to overcome. It's frustrating to feel like you have something great to offer when people don't know you're out there. And it's tempting to start looking at established people and wonder why it's so easy for them.

Comparison is an easy trap to fall into, especially when your business is just starting out. You may have other people whom you look up to and aspire to model your business after. It's great to have long-term goals, but comparing your progress with someone else's established career is not only unfair but detrimental to your success. It's easy to get discouraged when you're looking at someone's corner office from your corner-of-the-bedroom office, and you may start feeling like you'll never get there. It's like looking at a baby and saying, *Look at that dope, he can't even walk. What an idiot.* Your business is a baby right now, and you're starting from same place that all those successful people you admire did.

A while back, comedian Louis CK cut out the middleman on his tours. He didn't use Ticketmaster or rely on any outside promotion to sell seats. Instead, he just put the dates up on his website. He posted to various social-media networks that he was going on tour. Some press outlets picked it up, and word got around. Since this isn't a common practice with comedians at his level, the Internet was inundated with think pieces about a new touring model: booking things yourself without having to pay all the fees that go along with traditional promotion. But a lot of those articles were met with backlash—that model is great for someone with a huge audience like his, but what about the rest of us? He has, at the time I'm writing this, over 17,000 Twitter[1] followers to announce his new tour to. So what are us schmucks with a tenth as many fans to do? Many of the responses to Louis' tour were really bitter and seemed to suggest that he'd just woken up one day with all these people following him.

What they weren't considering, of course, is how he got that audience in the first place.

To look at him now, it seems obvious that he's so popular. He has a TV show and multiple successful tours and specials. He's on the late-night-talk-show circuit, and he does regular cameos for other shows. Of course he has 17,000 Twitter followers. You could look at all that and say, *Well, it's easy for him.* But he wasn't handed any of those things, and he didn't have many of them even ten years ago. He got all those things, and all those fans, in the same way that anybody else does: by touring and doing press and playing shitty clubs for tiny crowds for years. It may be easy for him to sell out a tour now, simply by mentioning that he's having one. But his plan would not have worked when he first started out.

---

1 CK has since closed his Twitter account, saying that it was a negative influence on his life, and replaced it with a Twitter account just for Louis CK news.

You can follow any famous band's trajectory to the same points. Take the Ramones, for example. You may not be a fan of the genre, but you've seen their logo, and you've probably heard several terrible covers of Blitzkreig Bop. Again, it's easy for them, right? Of course they have a ton of fans, they're the Ramones! They have a Grammy Lifetime Achievement Award, they're in the Rock and Roll Hall of Fame, everyone knows who they are. You can go to any mall in America and some kid is wearing their t-shirt. But at one point, they were just a couple of dudes playing bar shows for no money. They didn't just wake up one day and think, *We shall be a very famous band today*. There's not some governing body that awards you a fanbase.

They toured the globe relentlessly and developed a fanbase through hard work over twenty years, the same way that anyone does. This can seem like a bit of a letdown. Overnight-success stories are so prevalent, and you may be nurturing a little dream that once you tell the world about your service, your art, your product, your million-dollar idea, they'll just be banging down your door instantly. Then you can Scrooge-McDuck around in your money and scowl at paparazzi all day. But being successful in business isn't that glamorous. If you were hoping for some get-rich-quick advice, I don't have any. It takes work to reach those goals—a lot of work—sometimes over many years. The silver lining to this is that you can get there. These people you admire didn't just cross their fingers and luck into something that got huge. They built their empires with patience and persistence. They took incremental steps that you can take as well. This is why entertaining unfair comparisons is detrimental—looking only at where someone is now doesn't take into consideration where they started. As a brand-new band, you can't expect the kind of record and ticket sales that the Ramones were getting at the height of their popularity. But you can look at where they were when they had just started and use those benchmarks as more realistic goals.

Eventually, work begets work. You start out with a thing that feels like a boulder you're pushing. You're putting in all this work, but you're not getting much in return. You're always fighting to make some kind of headway, but you're slowly building your business, and all these bits that you're accomplishing start to fit together, and you keep building off that. When you're starting out, sometimes these bits don't seem like much. But eventually, people see what you're putting out there. Maybe they see a second thing you made, a third, a series, and maybe they decide to hire you for it. Maybe they even tell their friends, and suddenly you have this thing that has momentum. Say you've decided to start a business making cupcakes, but so far, your only clients are relatives. Still, your aunt mentions your cupcakes to her friend, who hires you for an event. You've posted some photos to Instagram, a friend sees them and recommends you to her boss for a company picnic. They both post photos to their own followers, and some more new people see your work. One of the followers is getting married and wants cupcakes for the wedding. The DJ there notices how great the cake is and starts recommending you to couples that are hiring him for their own weddings. All these things, on their own, are small. Some lead directly to jobs for you, and some don't. Some expose your work to people you may not have otherwise reached. Collectively, each of these small bits fits together to create a successful business.

This is how almost every overnight-success story goes. But you usually hear only the part in which the A&R guy shows up and says, *We've gotta make your record!* No one mentions the fact that this happens after the band has toured basements and VFW halls for eight years, that they've already generated some buzz locally and in a few press outlets, or that they have a moderately successful self-produced EP and a solid local fanbase. No one mentions this because a sudden "discovery" makes for a better story.

The Fest, in Gainesville, for example, is an independent music festival, started by Tony Weinbender of No Idea Records. More than 20,000 people descended upon Gainesville, FL, to camp out for the week for Fest 13, and it seems to take over more of the town every year, selling out before the event has even started for the past five years. Fest 12 hosted 400 bands over four days, and another 100 bands played over two days for the pre-Fest that goes on in Ybor City, FL. But when Fest started, back in 2002, numbers were significantly smaller. It started with only 60 bands at a two-day festival. It now has five times as many bands, another two days, plus the pre-Fest, and multiple venues. The growth has been steady and impressive, but it's come over many years. Organizers consistently put in work to book bands, set up venues, and advertise the event.

I've just passed the ten-year mark as a designer, and I am only recently getting some recognition for projects and getting opportunities like speaking at conferences and writing a book. I've been surprised by how long it can take to see returns on any one time investment. Sure, sometimes I'll post a piece that I've worked on, and, immediately, someone who has seen it will get in touch to commission something else from me. But the arc on a lot of returns has been significantly longer. Speaking at WMC Fest was a result of a chance I'd taken on volunteering three years before. The entire story of the Bobby Joe Ebola project is a process that took almost two years. People refer me to their friends based on projects that I'd done for them, sometimes several years ago. That A&R rep who shows up at an opportune time may have seen a demo that a band put out a few years back and only now had a chance to see them live. Just because you don't see an immediate response to what you're doing doesn't necessarily mean that people aren't noticing.

It's understandable (although really inadvisable) that people want to skip steps. Garry Tan wrote about how start-ups want to seem like big, established businesses, so they get the idea of imitating bigger companies. I've seen more than a few websites that talk of "we" and "the team" only to find out later that it's a one-person enterprise. Once, my husband's band booked a show at a venue called Planet of the Apes. Or, we thought it was a venue. It had an official-sounding name and a very nice website, which was more professional looking than some of the larger venues we had around town. After spending nearly an hour circling the same few streets, we realized that the three-car garage we were looking at was it. The goal was to make the place appear more official and established to bands looking for a place to play, which the owners accomplished. But our unrealistic expectations of what kind of venue it was, along with a lack of any representative photos, meant that we couldn't find the place, and we were really late loading in. It's common that a start-up wants to appear more established than it is, but pretending to be something you're not is no way to earn the respect of your customers, and in some cases, can lead to a really bad experience for them.

Sometimes, entrepreneurs want to skip steps so badly that they mimic even the bad habits of larger corporations—things like being indifferent toward their individual users, because that seems more professional, or being unnecessarily rigid in their policies, because that's how big corporations are expected to act.

In music, these are the bands that are aloof about their fans and act like divas about the lighting. They don't really care about the lighting, it's just that they think that's how big famous bands act. They think people will perceive them as A Big Deal if they act like A Big Deal. In reality, people just think they're dicks and don't want to work with them. On the other hand, I've seen bands that have an absolute blast doing things that they wouldn't be able to get away with if they were a huge band with tour buses and managers and bodyguards.

On Thrice's 2012 tour, Dustin Kensrue was performing after-show acoustic sets to benefit a charity called Invisible Children at several stops. They were very low-key affairs, and fans were alerted to the time and location via a tweet sent out about an hour before the set was to start. In Pittsburgh, they found a vacant basketball court on East Carson Street for the show. Dustin just stood on a wooden box in the middle of the court, playing guitar

"Everything (the only things) I know about business I learned from punk rock. A band, while it's almost never looked at this way, is like a small business. You have marketing and promotions, you are creating and selling a product, you have co-workers, and you need to manage money. The lessons learned from the successes and failures of those things are what I've applied to situations that arise in my day jobs, over the years, which have all been at small independent businesses. I am going to give away a big secret here: anything that you want to do but you don't think you'll be 'allowed' to do . . . just do it. And keep doing it till someone tells you to stop. Basement shows are the perfect example of this. That shit ain't legit, but kids keep doing it 'til they are forced to stop. World's Scariest Police Chases has benefited from this idea, as has Commonwealth Press. Another big benefit to flying under the radar is being able to fuck up and fail without being in a huge spotlight when it happens. Police Chases is a great example of a band filled with terrible ideas. Sometimes those terrible ideas go our way and work out great for us, other times it blows up in our faces, but we don't have a big spotlight on us, so it's not a big deal."

—Dan Rock, World's Scariest Police Chases

for the hundred or so folks who showed up. He didn't have security, barriers, or anything of that sort. He just showed up and played. After, he hung around to sign autographs and take photos. That's not something that Bono can get away with, at least not without starting a riot. But for most smaller bands, there aren't any rockstars. Once your band finishes the set, you become just a regular person, hanging out in the crowd with everyone else.

Of course, working within a large, established business (or a super-famous band) can have its perks, but there are advantages to being small, too. Being smaller allows bands to get closer to fans, and it allows businesses to get closer to customers. Instead of trying to skip steps, embrace where you are in your career. Use the advantages that being small can give you.

It may mean that you can offer much better customer service than a larger business would have time for, which gives you an opportunity for more meaningful and personal interaction with your customers. Or it may mean being the very best there is in a small niche, since you aren't worried about pleasing the majority, like a larger corporation has to be. It may be a personal touch that you can offer as a one-person shop, which a large company wouldn't be able to offer. Whenever I order records or merch from Tiny Engines (an indie record label based in the Carolinas), they send candy along with my order. Sometimes I'll see tweets from Commonwealth Press along the lines of *Whoever brings me coffee first gets a t-shirt*. That's not something that, say, Microsoft can do. *First person to bring Bill Gates a sandwich gets a copy of Windows 8*. Also, once I showed up to pick up an order of shirts that weren't done yet, so Dan gave me money to go get a milkshake while I waited. Staples is not going to buy me a milkshake because my order took longer than it said it would. But when you're small, you can do things like that and build a reputation with your customers.

Being small also means having the ability to be agile. One of the bigger downsides to working within a large company is that it takes a while to get anything done. You take your idea to your boss, then there's a meeting, and the results of that meeting go to a committee. There's another committee that reviews the work of the first committee, and paperwork to be filled out, and procedures that need to be followed. Several months later, your idea is almost a reality. As a one-person shop, I don't do any of that. I take my idea to my boss, which is me, and I think my idea is pretty great. I do some research on it, and if it looks like a good idea for my business, I make it happen.

This means that I get to be flexible with my customers. Often, couples get in touch with me about wanting custom packages for their weddings instead of what's listed on the website. Because I don't work for a large chain, I'm able to work out those requests on a case-by-case basis. I can treat customers uniquely instead of having to recite policies and guidelines that are decided by higher-ups. So I get to be closer to my customer. And when I do want to change a policy, or really any aspect of my business, I'm able to enact it immediately. I don't have a board of directors or VPs that I have to run it by. I don't have to take a vote.

It also means that if I have an idea for a promotion I want to run or new service I want to offer, I can run with it. Again, I don't have a marketing team to convince, and I don't have to get a PO through accounting before I can order buttons to sell at a show. I am accounting. And I am the marketing team. It means a lot of work for me, but also a great deal of autonomy. These are generally things that are very tough to accomplish with a big corporation, so take advantage of your current situation. You may not always be small.

SUCCESS!

BUILD YOUR OWN SPACE

So you're making things, you're building a great network of people, and you're embracing where you are in your career. You're doing what you can to make the world aware of your work, because, of course, people can't hire you or buy your product if they don't know that you exist. You may feel like you can't get your foot in the door to existing spaces. There isn't enough room in *Rolling Stone* for everyone, after all. And while there aren't gatekeepers to the Internet at large, there are still bigwigs with giant "rejected" stamps that can keep you out of their publications, their gated community, or their invite-only services. You may feel that spaces just don't yet exist for what you're doing—your product or service is so fresh that only a very small number of people are also offering it, or it's something that lacks a community to create spaces for it. In either case, you may need to make your own space.

Punk kids are pretty creative about making a space for themselves, usually out of the same necessity. While most major cities have huge arenas and a fair amount of midsize venues for established bands, there are generally far fewer places that welcome newer bands. Some that welcome newer bands won't book bands in a certain genre or won't host all-ages shows. Some kids live so far out in the boonies that there simply aren't any sanctioned venues at all. But how do you get to be an established band if there's nowhere for you to play and grow a fanbase? You make your own space.

Kids put on house shows in basements or garages. They rent out VFW halls, and many find even less-traditional spaces to turn into ad-hoc venues. World's Scariest Police Chases has played in warehouses, parking lots, and old churches. Thrash Fog played at an elementary school, in a hay field, and in an art gallery. Operation Ivy played at more than one laundromat. At Warped Tour, bands routinely set up their gear and play out of the parking lot, and I've been to multiple shows that have taken place in a field. Scott McMaster II of Ride or Die persuaded a friend's father to let him book shows in a building that he owned. The friend's father was having trouble renting out the building, which at the time was being used to hold coffins (he was a funeral director, and coffins need to be stored somewhere). McMaster and his friend used the building for two more years, usually holding shows every other weekend. They were able to build up a small scene in Youngstown, OH. The venue eventually grew into a space that others were using for their own purposes, including benefit shows and mixed-genre work. Anywhere a band can get a bit of space, electricity, and permission (optional) can be turned into a venue. There are plenty of aphorisms to apply here—*Necessity is the mother of invention* springs to mind. These ad-hoc spaces don't usually require much of a monetary investment, just someone willing to get out and create them. Once someone feels like he has the permission to create a venue, he can come up with some amazingly innovative solutions.

"Without a doubt my favorite performance ever was this illegal street show Violent Anal Death once played in Providence, RI. An anarchist bookstore hosted an all-day street concert with tons of local bands and asked us to close it out. By the time we went on, it was late at night, and there were cops converging, gathering at the edges of the crowd. There was just this electricity in the air, and I was having such a great time playing our set and interacting with the cops on the mic when suddenly I spied this guy I knew—we knew him as Larry Lips, and he was an older guy, a street guy, homeless I assume, and he had this sort of speech-tic kind of thing, maybe it was a form of Tourette's? He would always be talking and swearing under his breath about everything in the world. I would sometimes stop and talk with him. Get him a bagel or whatever. Anyway, here we were playing in this street, and we were so loud, at night it seemed extra loud, like you could hear the drums echoing off all the big buildings for blocks and blocks. And I was suddenly struck with this idea, so I motioned Larry over to the mic, and he came over. I handed him the mic and it was like a bomb went off. He started doing his usual talking but with the amplification it was like the whole city had to listen, and I started playing Paranoid by Black Sabbath and the other guys picked up on it and we just slammed through this perfect music moment with Larry Lips. Later on, a cop came over and borrowed the mic for a sec and read a statement that the mayor had declared this day "Free Music In the Street Day," so a bloody clash was also averted. Woo music!"

—Jason Chandler, Violent Anal Death / the Frustrators

Once, some friends planned a one-day battle-of-the-bands sort of festival. The biggest snag in getting set up was finding a space. We live in Podunk, where there's basically nothing. There was a small basement venue in the next town over, but there was no way it would hold enough people and bands for a whole day. There was no outside space to handle overflow and nowhere to eat (which meant that kids would have to leave), and the skirting-the-laws-of-physics maximum capacity was maybe 250 people. There was no venue where my friends could hold this thing. But one friend happened to work at the Taco Bell in town and somehow—I still have no idea how he got someone to sign off on this—his manager said that the group could put on an all-day festival in the parking lot. Of the Taco Bell. They got a flatbed truck out in the parking lot, made flyers, scheduled all the bands, set up the voting. They even had a dunk tank to make some extra cash to cover the costs. There were kids everywhere, loitering around, hanging out on the hillside, and buying as many burritos as they could carry (which must have been part of the pitch to the manager). For some reason, the the drive-thru was still open, so poor unsuspecting folks had to scream their orders over terrible grindcore bands. But the competition went reasonably well and was surprisingly organized. In fact, it went so well that the manager let them do it again the following year. So before you think you can't ask someone for some crazy thing that you want, ask yourself, is it weirder than having a concert in a Taco Bell parking lot? It never hurts to ask.

When the system isn't set up to work for you, then you need to work outside the system. You're allowed to question the way these things usually work and decide whether those methods make sense. Rather than complaining about how things should be, make them that way. Does a show have to be in a club? Does art have to be in a gallery? There's a t-shirt gallery show in Pittsburgh every year. Not only is it questioning whether t-shirts can be art (turns out, they can) but also what constitutes a gallery. Organizers just hang clotheslines up in a warehouse, and artists bring in shirts they've made to hang up. Boom. Gallery.

We're delving into finding that minimum viable product again, only this time we're looking at it from a marketing perspective instead of production. What do you need to get the word out, and where might you find it? What kind of space does this venture require? If it doesn't already exist, how can you make it exist?

Maybe you deal in antique furniture, and there's not a blog that features that sort of thing. Start one. The Internet makes carving out a space of your own in the digital realm increasingly easier to do. Setting up a website, a blog, a social-media account, even building a community in a virtual space, can be done inside of a day with little or no cost. If there isn't a space out there for you, you can be the person that starts one. But some endeavors require a physical space, and that can be a bit more complicated. When a local massage therapist couldn't find work at any of the nearby day spas, he teamed up with a local gym. He rented space there, and the gym referred business to him. He found a place that aligned with the services he offered and made a mutually beneficial deal with the business. He carved out a space for himself there. If your theatre troupe can't rent a stage for your production, what spaces are available that you could modify? What do you absolutely need to put on a show, and what spaces could possibly offer that? Evening Cure Productions built a stage at one end of an unused BMX bike room at a skate park and hosted shows there. It's non-traditional, but it had everything they needed.

Few businesses start out in a huge, shiny office or a sprawling studio space. Renting space is a large initial investment, and it eats up a big percentage of your profits. Home offices are an easy fix, and depending on the sort of work you do, can be really easy to accommodate. For writers, it may be just a small desk in a quiet space. Even if you're living in a shoebox-sized apartment, you can likely find that kind of space. Speaking of living in a shoebox-sized apartment, that's where I started my own business. I had a desk just big enough to fit a computer, which was in the living room/dining room of the apartment. I held meetings at local coffee shops, and I did all my photo shoots on location. But don't think that just because you're not doing computer-centric work, a home office isn't feasible for you. It may just require a bit more creativity.

Finding the space to open, say, an electronics-repair shop is hardly the same as finding the space to fit a computer in your home. Still, entrepreneurs, from bakers to screenprinters to fashion designers, have made work space in their own homes. Much to my husband's dismay, I've been using our kitchen table to do linoleum block prints for years. It's not an ideal setup, and working toward making some studio space in our home is certainly a goal of mine. But for now, I'm using what space is available to me and modifying it to meet my needs. For those who need more space than their homes can offer, co-working spaces are a good option. Co-working spaces are shared work environments that are independent of a single office or business and can bring together people in different industries. Sometimes, these spaces are simply open-plan offices where people can drop in and do their work around other people. TechShop offers access to tools like milling machines and lathes, welding equipment, woodworking equipment, and 3D printers, as well as safety and basic-use courses for processes that require it. Setting up that kind of space on your own would be significantly more expensive than a membership with TechShop, but you can have access to all those things for the cost of sharing a space with others.

Finding someone, or several someones, to share studio space with can make renting a place a more manageable solution. Some photographer friends have decided to share a studio space, since none of them do quite enough studio work to make independent renting cost-effective. They're able to cut their costs, but still reap the benefits of the space (not to mention sharing equipment, props, and studio furniture). Of course, you don't necessarily have to share spaces with people in your own industry. Sometimes these shared spaces can lead to unlikely housemates, who just happen to have similar space requirements. Spending time working with like-minded people, even if they're not doing the same sort of work as you, can foster a community. It gives you an opportunity to network with others who may be doing work that's related to yours—say, an interior decorator sharing space with a consignment buyer, or a designer sharing space with a commercial photographer. ABC No Rio houses a zine library, a darkroom, a silkscreening studio, a gallery, a public computer lab, and a venue. It fosters a community there, and many of the patrons' interests lie in more than one area. For those who want to develop some prints, read a few zines, and then see a show, it's a one-stop shop. The GoMedia building is home to a design firm, a recording studio, and a woodworking shop. It's unlikely that they originally intended to share space with people in those industries, but the building offered what each of them needed, and they turned out to be great neighbors. It may not be an obvious connection, or the first thing you think of, but being a little more open-minded can get you exactly the space you need.

When you get hired at a company, you're not going to have to find your own office space to work from; you just show up. Doing it yourself means that it's on you to find that space. A lot of bands realized early on that if they wanted to get their records out, they were going to have to do it themselves, so they started record labels. Jello Biafra of the Dead Kennedys had Alternative Tentacles; Brett Gurewitz from Bad Religion was running Epitaph out of his garage; Ian MacKaye and Jeff Nelson of the Teen Idles had Dischord;

Fat Mike of NOFX does Fat Wreck; Fang had one called Boner Records for God's sakes. There's a huge list of record labels that started just to get their owners' work out there but then grew into pretty successful businesses. However, nearly all of them started out of someone's house. None of these artists started a label and then immediately went out to rent office space, a giant warehouse, and a retail location. They started with what was immediately available to them—garage space—and they scaled up their physical space as they scaled up their businesses.

Epitaph, for one, has made itself into a household name but it started out as just a logo and a PO box. They pressed a record with a $1,000 loan from Brett Gurewitz's dad and sold 10,000 copies in a year, mostly through mail order. This wasn't a guy with a Harvard MBA and country club connections, this was just a guy that wanted to get his music out there, who got involved in something and found out that he had the skills to contribute to a community of people like him. Over the next thirteen years, Epitaph gew to become a breeding ground and landing pad for West Coast punk bands who wanted an international presence. One such band was the Offspring who had been together for ten years before releasing their third album *Smash* with Epitaph. The first single was played heavily on local radio and went on to sell eleven million copies, becoming the best-selling independent album of all time. Epitaph had six employees at the time. You learn a lot as you go. Epitaph had been largely ignored by the mainstream prior to 1994, but was now being contacted by major labels, who were telling them that they could not adequately support the Offspring's sales, offering to take the band off their hands. If Epitaph had started out as big as it is today, it would have been completely overwhelming. Figuring out distribution alone would be a daunting task. Instead, as most businesses do, the label started small and learned to scale. It's a big jump, but they were able to scale up existing operations.

Because of the success of *Smash*, Gurewitz quit Bad Religion and focused on the record label. These days, after 30 years of doing business, they have multiple offices, a few sister labels, and a lot more employees. They're no longer in a place where it's reasonable to run their operation out of a garage. They need space to house their wares and for employees to do their jobs. Figuring out exactly what you need to run your business is an important step, but you'll also need to constantly reevaluate that. Gurewitz also offers another lesson, how important it is to diversify your revenue. The Offspring comprised 95% of Epitaph's sales at that time, and despite efforts to renegotiate their contract, the band ultimately left for Columbia Records. The symbiosis had been magical and the band didn't do as well on Columbia with their next album only selling three million copies. Losing a huge client that accounts for the majority of your regular income can be devastating for a business, but it's not uncommon for newer ventures to lean too heavily on one big client. Ideally, you want to work to diversify your clients and broaden your income streams. As your business grows, your needs are going to change, and you have to repeat the same steps all over again. What do I need, and how can I get it?

When you create your own space, you get to make it your own. Whether it's physical or digital, you get to make decisions about how that space will be set up, how it will operate, and, in cases in which you're encouraging community involvement, how others are able to use it. When friends started venues, they had to figure out all those policies about how bands got paid, how money was dealt with, what kind of schedule they'd keep. Those that started labels may have begun just to get their own band's music produced, but many businesses grew into larger ventures. So they had to consider what sort of bands they would sign, how they'd handle marketing them, and how they'd pay out royalties. They had plenty of existing ventures that they could look to as a business model, but they didn't have to adopt those same policies. This was their space, and they could run it however they saw fit.

I had to do the same thing when I started doing photography. I had to care about things like what happens if someone cancels a shoot, a wedding gets rescheduled, or there's a tornado and I can't make it. Who holds copyrights, who has print rights, what does my contract say about family members that are uncooperative, what kind of usage rights does a band get? These aren't all things that I had a handle on the day I decided to start a business, but being a one-woman show, I get to change policies as needed. While all these things that you have to consider can seem intimidating, you get to create a business that runs the way you want, that treats customers how you want, and that operates in a way that aligns with your values. You get to change your rules based on your experience, and you get to make something that's yours.

	URGENT	NOT URGENT
IMPORTANT	DO THIS NOW. SERIOUSLY, PUT THE BOOK DOWN AND GET IT DONE.	MAKE A PLAN TO GET THIS DONE.
NOT IMPORTANT	DELEGATE THIS IF AT ALL POSSIBLE.	NOPE. GET THIS OFF YOUR LIST.

FIND YOUR JUGGALOS

I've had some major bouts with insomnia, which has resulted in my viewing a lot of infomercials. They always start in black and white, with some poor schmuck struggling through a mundane activity that I've never had any difficulty with. Then she's introduced to the pen with a magnetic cap, or a thing you stick to the floor of your shower to wash your feet with—finally! Her life is in color, she smiles, and at long last, she can fry an egg with ease. I'm always left to wonder, who is the target market? Where do they find people who are rushing to the phone for these products? And yet, these commercials persist, and I have to assume that someone, somewhere, is buying these products—that while I lie on my couch thinking, *who the hell would want a blanket with sleeves?* there's someone out there saying, *that is exactly the thing I need.*

A huge part of running a business is finding your market, your audience. You can have a cool idea and make a slick prototype, but if there isn't any interest in your product, then you don't have a business. You might make beautiful, handcrafted pager covers. But since pagers were widely replaced by smart phones, people aren't clamoring for artisanal pager accessories. You need to find those people who will see what you're offering and say, *yes, that. I need that.* Or, even better, *shut up and take my money.* These folks are called your target market. (Alternately, your people, your fans, your tribe, your customers.) These are the people that you want to reach, to market to, because they're the most likely to be interested in what you're doing.

The idea is to look for similarities in this group, to understand what sort of people like your product or would use your service. Maybe most of your customers are men, or librarians, or families with small children. You may find that your people have similar values, or live similar lifestyles, or are of similar ages. Or that people interested in your business are also interested in the same other products, in the vein of Amazon's "people who bought x also bought y" recommendation system. Once you figure out what kind of people are interested in your business, you can figure out where those people spend their time and attention, and then you know where to reach them. If your target market is women over 40, an advertisement in *GQ* is likely to be a waste of your money. If you're trying to reach young, recent college graduates, then *Yacht Owners Weekly* would similarly be a poor choice. A death-metal band is unlikely to get a warm reception at a folk festival. You get the idea. You'll spend a lot of time, especially in the early part of starting your business, trying to get in front of people who are likely to become your customers. It makes sense to aim for places where your demographic is likely to see you.

You can get pretty niche with your target market, say, *my customers are vegan bicyclists that live in a major metro area* or *we're targeting retired circus performers.* Or in the case of my *Firefly* posters, *my customers are REALLY into a sci-fi show that got cancelled a decade ago.* A niche clientele helps you to narrow down your marketing, but it's also a limited group. If you get too small a niche, you may not have the customer base you'll need to sustain a business. *Women ages 30-32 named Amanda who live in the south and also raise lemurs* may be a niche that contains only one person—maybe get a little less specific. But many new entrepreneurs struggle with the opposite, insisting their product is for everyone. It's an easy trap to fall into, I mean, who *wouldn't* want to buy this thing? And it may even be technically correct; anyone could buy one of my posters. There's nothing about a poster that limits the demographic by age or gender or socioeconomic status (or really any demographic identifier). But your target market isn't only people who are technically capable of purchasing your product or hiring you for a service. It's the people that are *likely* to do so. If your target market is *everyone*, you're doing it wrong. And you should also probably look up what "target" means.

"We had the idea to print yardage to make large-scale stretched-canvas pieces. When we calculated the price that we'd have to sell them for—it just didn't make sense. We didn't think anyone would buy them. We just wanted to see if we could actually execute it successfully, so we printed some fabric and made one, as a personal project. We dropped it off at Art All Night (a twenty-four-hour event in Pittsburgh where anyone can submit a piece of art). When the event was over, we had over two-dozen bids on our piece. Most were in the price range that we were thinking and we realized that there was a market for what we wanted to make. We sold that piece and probably over 50 more. While we've stopped making those pieces, we were really happy that they were a success and that we were able to make them and still make a little money." —Becki Hollen, Everyday Balloons

There's a reason that most of the punk shows I attend have similar tables set up with pamphlets and petitions for various social causes—the type of people who listen to that music are typically also interested in said social causes. There's an overlap in that Venn diagram. It makes sense that those organizations reach out to people who are likely to embrace their message, and they've figured out where those people hang out. Of course, this isn't a guarantee. While there are people who are there just for the band and don't give half a crap about PETA or Greenpeace, there might be only one person at a Toby Keith concert who would care very much about those organizations. The percentage is much higher at the former event than the latter, and tabling at a place with a 70-percent success rate is a better use of time and resources.

Going back to those previous examples, there may be a few 40-year-old women reading *GQ* and a few college graduates who are also proud yacht owners, but even if a publication reaches a very large audience, how many people in that audience will also have any interest in what you're doing? It may sound like a great deal, to run an ad that could be seen by 100,000 people. But if those 100,000 views translate to just one interested person, then is it really such a good deal after all? You may have paid thousands of dollars for an ad to get one good lead. This is the problem with the shotgun-blast approach to marketing— you're reaching a lot of people, but you're reaching a lot of people who don't care about your business. If you're using a more targeted approach, you may reach only 100 people. But out of those 100 people, 80 of them may contact you, because you put in the time to figure out where your people are. It's a much better return on your money.

Not everyone will like your product. Not everyone will use your service. Not all people will see how your business is relevant to their lives. If you spend your time trying to cater to everyone, you're likely to end up with something that nobody's interested in. Figure out who your people are, and care about just those people.

To illustrate this point, I want to talk about Insane Clown Posse. While they may not be punk, they are suing the FBI, which is pretty punk rock. That aside, these guys know their audience. They don't understand how magnets work, but they're amazing at marketing. You might think their band is terrible and ridiculous and stupid. You know who don't care? Insane Clown Posse. They don't care because you aren't their audience. They're not for everybody, and hey, these clowns get that.

But they are for some people. In fact, some people don't only like this group, they are rabid and loyal fans. ICP have inspired grown adults to wear clown makeup and JNCO jorts, call themselves Juggalos, and spray Faygo pop at each other. That's how much people relate to and love them. For the better part of 1994, ICP passed out flyers to their free shows, wearing trenchcoats and face paint. They were mostly laughed at or ignored while their black cube truck was parked outside, literally painted with images of clowns. Despite the public reaction—to mock nearly everything about them—they stuck to it and found their demographic. They kept throwing up their flag for anyone that related to them, and suburban teenagers came out by the millions to support them, wearing clown makeup and carrying two-liters of Faygo.

There are people who will think your work is terrible and stupid, and these are not your people. I'm not saying you should ignore criticism about your business or shrug it off as people who "don't get you." But some people really won't get you, and you shouldn't automatically assume that all criticism or negative reviews lobbed your way are valid.

It's possible those critiques are coming from people who will never be interested in your business. For Insane Clown Posse to put out a record that I actually enjoy, they'd have to change so drastically that they'd retain almost none of their existing fan base. They can't afford to care about making me happy. Their music is simply not for me, and my complaints aren't—shouldn't be—important to them. They understand their target market—those folks with crates of Faygo on standby. And ICP aren't wasting any of their time trying to cater to people like me, who don't fall into that target market. That's time they could be spending making a new album, planning a tour, or selling their merch to people who already love them.

What you need to do is find your Juggalos—those people who are just nuts about what you do, who will tell their friends how amazing you are, who come to your shows or buy your prints. Find those people and get your work in front of them. Listen to their feedback critically, because these are the people who support you. Criticism from someone who's never in a million years going to be your customer isn't nearly as valuable as criticism from a fan.

Keeping something simple can be a difficult undertaking. Really sticking to your vision and not tacking on bells and whistles that might draw in more customers takes confidence. This can be a really hard thing to do—there are always more functions that you could introduce into your product or service. Any software engineer will tell you that adding in more things to appeal to more people often results in a bloated program that alienates your core users. Trying to accommodate every user request often means killing what made that product so good to begin with. People who make that mistake have lost sight of their target market and of their product goals. Know what your audience needs, know what makes your business work, and learn to let go of the idea of pleasing everyone.

You also want to make sure that your fans can get to you. Starting out, many bands have young fans and a fundamental problem in getting their music to the kids that wanted to hear it—kids under twenty-one couldn't attend shows because they couldn't get into bars. Bands couldn't play for their Juggalos. They couldn't get their music in front of the people who would really appreciate it. They had to find a workaround, and many opted simply not to play in bars. They put on all-ages shows in spaces like veterans' halls and rec centers and high-school gyms. In communities that lacked underage venues, bands could have simply thrown up their hands at the situation. Instead, they asked, *what can we do about this?* They offered to card people at the door and mark a big "X" on the hands of underage kids so that the bar would know whom not to serve. The clubs agreed, and young punk fans got to attend shows.

You want to make sure that your Juggalos can get to you. Does your target demographic use Android phones, but your game runs only on iOS? Your Juggalos can't get to you. Do the people who love your handmade quilts live overseas, but you don't ship internationally? The people who want to support you can't. It doesn't help to find your audience and then market your business to people who aren't able to access it. You can't cater to every demographic, so cater just to the people who love what you do.

"The DIY ethos in most of the punk scene I was a part of inspired me to just start stuff. To make something out of nothing. And the most important thing was the authenticity of the voice behind it more than the quality of the product. Of course, I always got hung up on the quality of my work. I was kind of a perfectionist and wouldn't put out something I wasn't proud of. But the DIY ethos helped me feel brave to start new things and build stuff from the ground up."
—Jeff Finley, Go Media and Campfire Conspiracy

I had some trouble with this when I first started working in wedding photography. A lot of people knew me for taking photos of bands or for drawing nonsense like skateboarding anthropomorphic pizzas. But I spend a lot of my time shooting weddings, which I also love doing. Of course, when I started, I read a lot of the major wedding blogs and magazines, and most of them had the same kind of tone—very gushy, very flowers-and-rainbows, and that's just not how I talk. I've never said "eyegasm" in my whole life, and I feel sort of gross typing it. But when I started a blog of my work, that was how I wrote—in my posts, in my policy pages—I wrote how I thought a wedding photographer was supposed to, instead of writing like me. I did fine. I had some great clients, some okay clients, and some clients who were probably a bad fit. I could have probably continued getting mostly okay work that way, but I felt disingenuous. People would read my blog and get a certain impression, we'd set up a meeting, and I'd show up. I was probably not what they were expecting, which was entirely my fault. Worse, one of the things I stress to people when I meet them is that they should hire a photographer whom they like and get along with, because that's the only vendor you're stuck with all day. If you think your florist is a jerk, you can pick up your flowers and never talk to that guy again. But you'll be stuck with me for ten or twelve hours.

I'm preaching this to people, that you should get to know your photographer and find one you get on well with, yet all of the things that I'm posting are in no way helping them to do that. So I dropped it. I rewrote my policies and contracts, and going forward, I just wrote like myself. I was authentic in my blog posts about my shoots. I set up policies to reflect the way that I thought things should work, not how other wedding photographers were doing it. Now, I get awesome clients. I get the type of people I want to work with, and they get the type of photographer they want. Insane Clown Posse taught me to be authentically myself, even if I'm kind of weird and mouthy. Because there are people out there who will be really into my authentic, weird, mouthy self. A bride once explained to me that she'd chosen to hire me specifically because I wasn't "bubbly"—she'd found all the other photographers she'd met with to be exhausting. It's beneficial to your business and to your clients to represent yourself honestly.

Even though I'm not super flowery about it, I really do love shooting weddings. I have incredibly cool people contact me, and they're going to be a little family of cool people together. It's the best. I love capturing all that. If you want to make something that sticks with people, you need to make something that you can get behind. Because part of your job, no matter what it is that you do, is to persuade people to hire you to do that thing. This is known as hustlin'. You want them to book your band, publish your novel, buy your cupcakes, or hire you to care for their kids. And it's harder to sell people on something that you don't believe in—you need to be a convincing actor on top of being a successful small-business owner. People can tell if you're phoning it in. Authenticity matters, even to people in clown makeup.

I'm not actually going to talk about sellouts here, because I think that's as boring as arguing over who's punk and who's not. Money is kind of a taboo subject in the punk scene, and some small-business owners get a little squirmy when you get into the subject, too. While the punk community has taught me so many positive things, it's also taught me a few things not to do. The subject of money actually puts a few points into each column. I learned a little bit about good money management from touring bands but a lot about an extremely negative attitude toward money, which will be destructive to your business.

It's amazing to me how many bands will jump to touring (and how many entrepreneurs will throw themselves into a new business) without doing any math first. This seems to be a pretty basic concept, but you want to have a solid understanding of how much this undertaking will cost you versus how much you'll be bringing in. You want to have some kind of budget, which you'll likely need to revisit at various points to make sure you're still on track. And you want to have these things before you take that leap.

One method to keep your cash flow in the black is one that Adam Joad touched on in a previous chapter—keeping your overhead low. A rather ridiculously named band wrote an article detailing how they'd made some $136,000 on tour but still lost money. This is because the expenses for that tour were close to $148,000. Now, this is fairly basic math, but I'm gonna help you out—they spent $12,000 more than they made. Clearly, they didn't bother to do that basic math before they lined up equipment rentals, lighting boards, and huge tour buses. These things might be really nice to have, but they apparently aren't things you can afford right now, Ridiculously Named Band. If, on the other hand, you decide to head out with just your band and a merchandise person in a van, which you'll also be sleeping in, you won't need nearly as much cash to keep your bank account positive. You'll have to cut luxuries to afford necessities like gas and food.

Likewise, when I started out in photography, I didn't immediately rent a studio and hire employees. With just me, working out of my home, I didn't have much overhead, and it didn't take as much income to make the business financially successful. Bootstrapping is your friend, particularly when you're just starting out. It's easy to get weighed down thinking *I need an office, I need to be in the city, I need a dozen employees and state of the art equipment to even think about starting this thing*. You don't. You don't necessarily need fancy equipment to make something cool. When I say I run a small business, I mean a *really* small business— it's just me. It's incredibly important to identify those things that you honestly do require to succeed, and those things that you don't. Would owning a huge studio with an office space make me feel super important? Maybe. But am I in a position that it would help my business? No, I'm not. It would require me to raise my rates to offset the cost, but since most of my work is on location, it wouldn't really help me to bring in more business. Now, do I need a solid camera for my photography business? Yes, I definitely need that, and that's where I'm going to spend my cash. I learned to keep my overhead low, because it makes it easier for me to keep my business running. I learned to buy new equipment only if I could justify that my current gear was holding me back. Is this purchase going to save me enough time to justify the expense? It's important to look as critically at your expenses as at your income sources.

Don't go into debt to buy equipment if you can help it. You may be in a position where taking out a loan to start your business is a necessary course of action—if you're opening a gym, you'll have to rent space and buy machines, and there are some large startup costs. But try to figure out your MVP—*what's the least that I can start this business with, without giving up crucial elements*—and start with that. Whatever you have, scope it down to something you can ship. Show it to your friends, talk about it, give it a platform. Use that to earn the cash to put back into your business. I found some advice on the first year of business as a photographer, and it read, "a laptop won't do it. Don't even try, you need a powerful processor." I wasn't in a place where I could afford a new computer that met all their recommended specs. As I mentioned, all I had was a very old laptop that was an absolute time bandit, but was still technically able to run the software that I needed. I was really insistent about not putting things on credit, and I also made sure that I made business purchases with only business funds (not from my own personal checking account). I kept saving money from my photography work until I could afford to upgrade to the gigantic cinema-screened beast that I use today. It's very easy to blame your gear for your not getting started—*I can't do this because I don't have a new Mac Pro or this software or that camera or this much studio space*. I've made flyers with a Xerox machine, and I worked for a whole year using a lens that wouldn't autofocus on my camera, so I shot hockey with a prime lens, manual focus. This is the photographer equivalent of walking to school in the snow, uphill both ways. Is it harder to do? Of course. But it's not impossible.

You're ready now. Figure out how to take what you have today, and start.

Figuring out your minimum overhead helps stem the tide of money going out, but what about increasing the money coming in? Consider how to get passive income to work for you. Everyone hits that roadblock of having only so many workable hours in a day, but bands on tour have only the length of their set—anywhere from fifteen minutes to an hour—to get paid for the thing they actually do. There's a set door price and a set time limit, and the venue has agreed to pay them so much for that time. That's all the money they can make there. Eventually, the amount may be higher—they're headlining instead of opening, tickets may cost more—but it's still capped there. Unless, of course, they had something else to offer people.

Welcome to merch. Bands have t-shirts, stickers, back patches, records, pins. They will create a great experience in their live shows and then embed that experience in real products that all remind you of said show. All those things take time to make, but once they've made them, it takes significantly less time to reproduce them. That's how passive income works. You're effectively selling something that you don't have to put much additional time into. I do custom design work for all manner of projects, and my time on that is capped. I can work only so many hours in a day. However, I have personal projects that I've made and can continue to sell. I made some posters, I have a few t-shirt designs, I have some linoleum block prints, and they're all available in an online shop. The first one took time—I had to make an illustration or carve a block. But now, I have a stack of posters and shirts and prints in stock. While I'm minding my business and doing other work, people purchase them. I can keep selling that same design, but with custom work, I get paid only once. While this may seem like an easier thing to do for maker types, people in service industries can do the same thing. Many venues will rent out space on off nights, which requires very little work or time commitment on their part. Photographers, bakers, or consultants might offer e-books to share knowledge that's of interest to clients and colleagues. It takes time to create that guide, but once you complete it, you can continue selling it indefinitely.

Of course, you'll need money to create all these pieces, and where does that come from? Your business fund. In the interest of not losing everything you own, it's important to separate your own money from business money. Most of my friends in bands had a band fund, which wasn't any individual's money, but, collectively, it was the band's money. As such, it was spent on band things.

I worked awhile without having a business account, because I thought it'd be easy enough to keep my money separate. Maybe you're better at that than I am, but I found it really helpful to have a separate account just for business. I developed a system: when I got paid for a job, I'd split the money three ways. A certain percentage went into my main checking account—so I'm paying myself. A percentage went into the business account, for taxes, because I'm at a point in my life where all my income is untaxed, which can make for some unpleasant surprises come April if you're not prepared. The rest went into the business account, for use on the business—if I needed to buy a new lens or some postcards for marketing mailers, that's where the money would come from.

So, using the band model, say you get your guarantee from a venue. You do your three-way split and then look at what's in the band fund. Since some of your income goes to reinvesting in your band, some of that money can be used to buy t-shirts. (Maybe some goes to replacing an amp that blew out. Some methods of reinvesting don't result in new income. And certainly there are expenses like gas and food.) The next time out, you can add that t-shirt money to the income you're guaranteed, and at the end of the tour, you do your split again. This time you're making shirts again, but some of that money gets invested in making a record, and you keep on that way. Some of your income should always be going to making your business better. Passive income streams are one of the ways you can do that.

All this talk about money might sound terribly crass to you. You're following your passion and creating something that speaks to you, and you're not going to sully that with talk about money. The thing is, money matters in a business. If you want to do this as a hobby, then there's a whole different set of rules. You can do whatever you want. You can go on tour at your own expense and not make a dime. You can give away paintings. You can set up workshops and teach for free. But if you want to make a living at any of it, then money matters. Ira Glass, host of *This American Life,* said that the more idealistic you are about your work, the more savvy you have to be about the business side. Because you're doing something you love and you're making something that you want people to see, it's a lot more tempting to take any opportunity to work, even if the pay is terrible or nonexistent. If I'd been told that the pay would be really low at the jersey factory where I used to work but that it'd be really good exposure, there is zero chance I would have even considered taking that job. I would have laughed my way out of the interview because it wasn't something I was personally invested in, and the paycheck was my only motivator. They weren't offering me anything *but* money.

When you're working on something you feel strongly about, though, something that you feel is important to get out into the world, there are benefits other than money. This certainly makes it a lot harder to decide whether an opportunity is worthwhile. The decision is harder but also incredibly important in order to determine what sort of exceptions you're willing to make. Is bartering with another business something you're willing to consider? Are there conditions under which you're willing to work for free? Some writers will publish unpaid work only on their own blogs because, at the very least, traffic earned is to their own platform, instead of someone else's. When people offer me exposure in lieu of payment, I remind them that people die of exposure. But I am willing to do *pro bono* (that's Latin for "free") work for certain charities. You're able to work outside standard business practices if you want to, but it's also important to remember that most of the world doesn't. You can't pay your rent with Instagram likes or a really cool scarf. Make sure you're bringing in enough actual money for your business to operate.

It's easier to be taken advantage of when you care so much about your work, and it's a problem that's compounded by the guilt some people have over making money at all. Some feel like they shouldn't be making money for doing something that they love and enjoy, that the work should be its own reward.

In the punk scene, there's an attitude that if you *do* make money doing something you love, it will make your work inauthentic, and you will be a terrible sellout. It's a really strange attitude. Say I'm a fan who loves your band. You make amazing music, and it's the best thing I've ever heard, but I can't give you any money for making it because it's art, and you should be doing that just for the love of doing it. You can't get day jobs either, though. When would you have time to write and practice and record all this amazing music that I love? Plus, you won't be able to get time off from work to go on tour to Podunk. And even if you were to keep making the exact same music, which I adore, if you sign to a major label, or make any money, or if, God forbid, other people find out who you are and you get popular, I'm going to tell everyone what sellouts you are. Did I say I loved your band? What I meant is, you're the worst.

There's a serious backlash in response to any kind of success. The punk police come out of the woodwork. *This is punk, but that isn't. This makes you a sellout, and that doesn't.* They're some of the most boring people to be around. Eventually, when some bands did start actually making some cash and touring in buses instead of vans, they'd hear, *You can't come back to us if this doesn't work out.* How many years do you have to live in a van and eat at soup kitchens? Are you ever allowed to make a living at this? People can somehow be a huge fan of what you're doing but still expect you to live in abject poverty while you do it, or else whatever you're making isn't authentic. It's not art if you get paid for it.

People who grow up around this mindset can have a hard time shaking it, and they carry it into their business ventures, even when they're entirely unrelated to that scene. It's an attitude that is counterproductive to running a successful business, for obvious reasons. You don't have to sell your soul or ditch all your values to make a living. But you do need to develop a healthier attitude about getting paid.

I may have a different perspective on this than some, having studied graphic design, which is considered a commercial art. Naturally, I feel that being a commercial art doesn't necessarily preclude graphic design from also being a fine art or an authentic expression.

Let's talk for a minute about the Sistine Chapel. I did my undergraduate thesis on papal portraiture and am morally obligated to talk about Renaissance artwork as often as possible. I bring it up because Michelangelo got paid to create the famous mural on the chapel's ceiling. In fact, he got paid Pope money, which means he got paid extremely well to create it. That sweet paycheck was his driving motivation to even take on the work—Michelangelo considered himself a sculptor and thought that painting was kind of beneath him, and he was actually really busy with another sculpting project at the time. But Julius II was insistent and willing to compensate him for his time, so Michelangelo went ahead and painted the ceiling.

Are we really going to accept the punk scene's easy argument that this isn't art because he was paid for it? Or it isn't art because he got paid really well for it? Or that it isn't art because it was client work? It sounds entirely ridiculous. And yet, by that very black-and-white definition in which making a living from your work negates the work itself, the Sistine Chapel panels are not art, are not authentic, and Michelangelo is a sellout (so you should probably start telling your friends that you really like only his older stuff).

You may, understandably, not be comfortable with equating whatever work you're doing with one of Michelangelo's most famous masterpieces. But you can do authentic work that speaks to people in a real way, with integrity, and also make a living from your efforts. The two are not mutually exclusive. It's a mindset you need to fully embrace if you have plans to run a successful business.

"Dog Days was terrible about money management. When we regrouped, we were just happy to be playing again. We recorded our full-length and knew things were different. Things were slower, and we weren't serious about being a full-time band. We made our music free. We gave it away on Bandcamp, and, out of my own personal obsession, I printed 50 packaged CDs. We figured, why not get it to as many people as possible? Not a bad idea, unless you want to see a return for the work you put in. I know there will be some of you out there that say 'man, making music should be for the love, not the money.' You're half right.

"You should make music for the love, but making money at something you're good at shouldn't be looked down upon. If you have something people want, sell it. As an audience, we should want to support the people that give us something special in life. Giving money to bands that give me music that betters my life is no sweat. They deserve it. Where would I be without the bands that I grew up on? What if Bad Religion couldn't fund their albums? Who would I be if the bands I saw when I was younger couldn't tour because they couldn't afford to?

"How you run your band is—and totally should be—up to you. I'm curious to see where the music industry goes when there are a million bands getting paid nothing for creating music?"   —David Wilson, Skies Bleed Black / Dog Days

Now, I may have leaned a little hard on Michelangelo's taking the gig only for the money. We've all been there, Mike. But once he accepted the job, he went on to argue with Pope Julius II about the content of the painting and negotiated a much bigger project, as well as a way more complex piece. If he was going to do this damn ceiling project, he was going to do it right.

"The Punk and DIY scene taught me that money is evil. This isn't a good lesson, but rather a belief system that doesn't exactly make it easy to make money. When you think money is evil and you don't want to be greedy, you make it hard for yourself to charge what you are worth. You discount too much. You undersell yourself. You have a skewed perception of money from listening to too many anarcho, anti-capitalist, hippie punk bands. This belief led me into situations where I was always trying to justify my prices to the 'punx' of the world and constantly being afraid of being called a sellout. And this caused a lot of conflict in me as I tried to make sense of it amidst questioning and criticism from outsiders. I learned what 'working for exposure' was all about. That exposure was considered an acceptable form of payment for doing any kind of work for the music business. I fell for it many times and had my fair share of exposure. I was even published in national magazines. I've learned that exposure does not equal happiness and doesn't put food on my plate. Exposure alone isn't worth it."

—Jeff Finley, Go Media and Campfire Conspiracy

DO WORK,
GET PAID.

Don't half-ass it. Don't ever.

I know it's tempting. You're on a deadline to get something out, and it's good enough. You're working with a difficult client, and it's easier just to do whatever is asked of you, even if you know it's a bad idea. I'm not going to say that I've never sent out something I wasn't 100% proud of into the world, because I'm sure I could dig up something. But it's rare, and I put a lot of hours into keeping it that way. It's easy to think at the time that it's just one client, just one project, just this one time. But you can't ever know who's going to see that one thing, and in the age of the Internet, nothing ever really dies. That one project may be the only thing a potential client sees before making a decision about what kind of business you're running.

Way back when they were first starting out as a band, Green Day booked a show on some godforsaken mountaintop. If you're at all familiar with the band, you've likely read this story before. This show was in the middle of nowhere, in a house with no roof, where about five kids bothered to show up. This wasn't an ideal show. This was the sort of show where you want to call your people and see if someone can fake laryngitis so you can get out of playing it. It was the sort of show that you show up for and treat like a practice. They didn't. Instead, they put on the best show that they could. As it happened, in addition to the handful of kids that made it out, Larry Livermore was present. Larry co-owned Lookout Records, which put out Green Day's first two albums. Of course, I can't argue that even if they had totally blown off that show, they might still have become gigantically famous. But there's no way to know, much like there's no way to know whether that one time you phoned it in could have been a huge opportunity for you.

Word of mouth is a huge deal, especially when you're starting out. Even if you're not playing for some A&R rep that'll eventually make you famous, you've gotta put your best work out there, because that one kid who showed up might have turned out to be your biggest fan. Maybe that kid comes to all your shows, buys all your records, and tells her friends. Then her friends come to all your shows and buy your merch, too. But she's only going to do that if you put on a show—a real show, one you're not half-assing because there are only five kids there or the bass player's pissing you off or playing at VFW halls is beneath you. Blow those five kids away. Make them tell their friends that they missed the best show ever.

And yes, you can replace "band" with "business" in this little story. Maybe someone finds your illustration on a billboard, your article in a magazine at a doctor's office, or a post on your blog through a Google search a year from now. You have no idea who is going to see your work. People have referenced some really old work of mine when hiring me. In fact, I had a couple hire me to shoot their wedding based on photos they'd seen from my trip to Costa Rica. In 2004. Which is not in any way featured, or even mentioned, on my photography website. People will find that one project you put out and then never thought about again.

The way you treat people is just as important as the work you're doing when it comes to building a reputation. Maybe one of your past clients tells friends about the quality of service you provided. You're not there to explain that you had this really tight deadline, and the client was like . . . the worst, and you were having a bad day, and you know, it's just not really your best work. To potential clients looking at that piece or hearing that story from a friend, that's you. They don't have any other context for you—as a person or a business—and they're not obligated to give you the benefit of the doubt. They'll just find someone else. To them, that's who you are, and that's the kind of work you do. That's the way you treat your customers. So make sure every project is something you can stand behind.

If you're in any sort of service industry, someone is always contracting you out. Have personal goals for outside assignments. There's a thing I learned when shooting for newspapers. It's that you always get your editor the shot. Always. Don't mess that part up. Whatever you're being contracted to do, make sure you meet those base expectations. But think about what you want to get out of it, too. Set higher standards for yourself than other people set for you.

I was asked to shoot a local band for *Pittsburgh City Paper*, the Bastard Bearded Irishmen. Now, my editor there is a pretty cool artist herself, so she's always happy to get interesting things. But it's still a newspaper, with deadlines, and she would probably have been fine with getting just a shot with everyone in focus. F8 and show up, as they say. But I looked at the assignment as an opportunity for me—what do I want to get out of this

"Everything about being a DIY punk kid from Western PA means going above and beyond. Have a band? Might as well start a label to release the records, and get a Roboto membership to book the shows. Work in a warehouse? Might as well build a venue in the back. I'm constantly surprised when I meet people that don't think this way. World's Scariest Police Chases is pretty much the only band I've ever seen flyer for their [Gainesville, FL] Fest set. How is that possible?

"It was to be our 4th show, at Fest, a gathering of 300 or so of the best punk bands around. We knew no one would know who we were, and we needed some way to set ourselves apart and get people interested.

"We made flyers that said we were members of Dillinger 4, Latterman, and Lawrence Arms, and just for good measure we included a Fat Wreck Chords logo. Why not, right? We covered Gainesville in posters and handed out flyers, and by the time we were ready to play, the place was packed. We won an award from *Alternative Press*. Our friends were freaked out, they thought we were going to get sued or something (by who? Fat Mike? That dude's got enough going on). It was pretty funny. Kids were buying our merch before we even played. I thought it was a good scheme to get people to show up, but I thought it would almost definitely backfire once kids realized we lied to them and they'd hate us, but much to my surprise, they got stoked and were totally into it. Total win. The only bummer part, which we didn't realize at the time, was that the band after us actually *did* have members of Latterman, but no one realized, and the audience left after our set . . . oops?

"The next day we saw Dan Yemin (Lifetime, Kid Dynamite, Paint it Black) on the street and he told us, 'Hey, I saw your shitty punk band yesterday. It was cool. Reminded me of that shitty band Bad Brains.' I'll take that weird fucking compliment any day of the week.

"To this day, there are still times our band is mentioned on the Internet somewhere and someone will say, 'Oh yeah, that's the band with guys from D4, Lawrence Arms, and Latterman right?'

"I can't tell you how many cool opportunities we've gotten at Commonwealth Press from customers who know we always bust our asses for anything we get involved in. When we started working with Penn Brewery, we mentioned to them that we had always wanted to make our own beer. As soon as they heard that, they said if we were going to make a beer, they wanted to be involved. We were working with Joe Grushecky when he came to us and asked us to design and print the t-shirts, posters, and passes for his show with Bruce Springsteen. We couldn't just play the Fest, we had to get involved to the point that Commonwealth Press now prints every Fest t-shirt and hoodie that they sell. Work hard, be nice, be fair, and cool shit will happen. It's that simple."

—Dan Rock, World's Scariest Police Chases and Commonwealth Press

photo? So instead of getting just the bare minimum that was asked of me, I treated this thing like I was shooting the cover of *SPIN*. I did a ton of research and planning to make it a cooler shoot than it had to be. I found out that they had played their very first show in the produce section at a Giant Eagle, so I spent most of a day making phone calls to see if the grocery store would be open to letting us shoot there (and received several very confused *nos* from various employees). I took the request pretty high up the Giant Eagle ladder but was informed that the company just doesn't allow that sort of thing. In a lot of cases like this,

I'm a "beg forgiveness rather than ask permission" kind of girl. But they're an Irish band, there are seven of them, and the shoot would require bringing in lighting gear, and it wasn't the sort of thing we could just sneak in and get a few quick shots while people picked out tomatoes. So that was a bust.

But we called around to a few other places that could work, and I talked to the band about what kind of shot they wanted. We ended up doing the shoot in a tattoo shop, where one member pretended to get the band's logo tattooed onto his chest. Justun, who runs In The Blood Tattoo, where we shot, made a stencil out of their logo and sat in to pretend-tattoo it for the photo. I could have just lined them up somewhere around Pittsburgh and gotten the bare minimum the paper needed. I'd have gotten paid, and the paper would have run the boring photo, and that would be that. Instead, they got to run a more interesting photo, I got a more interesting photo for my portfolio, and the band got a shot that better shows their personalities. And, to my point, I sent out into the world a piece of work that I'm proud of, instead of something subpar I find myself giving bullshit excuses for. And also I got paid.

Pittsburgh City Paper has since hired me again. If I would have turned in a boring shot that I didn't put much effort into, or if I had been a pain to work with or was late delivering the photo, my odds of getting rehired would have gone way down. I've heard, in this line of business, that you're only as good as your next shot. I'm not knocking that. You should always strive to do better, not just rest on a really cool thing you did a few years ago. But your last shot, and, more importantly, the attitude with which you handled that last shot, can make or break you.

This concept doesn't apply to just your output—the thing you make or the service you offer. It applies to the way that you deal with people, how you handle your customer service and your business relationships. Your laziness will hurt your business. Not researching clients before you email them the same lame, generic pitch that you're sending to every game in town will hurt your business. Bad customer service, like not returning phone calls, not keeping your customer in the loop, or sending out poorly timed surveys, is bad for your business.

My husband had some car trouble (it stopped moving, which we both view as a pretty essential car function), but luckily we have roadside assistance to call for a tow truck and schedule the car for service. The company called to ask him to do a customer-satisfaction survey minutes after they had picked up his car. I'm sure it's easier to knock these things out quickly, but this is the worst possible time to contact someone. He's still angry that his car isn't working, and he hasn't even spoken to a mechanic to see what the damage will be. Of course he isn't satisfied. If the company had been using its whole ass when it decided on how this system would run, it may have given more thought to the customer's experience. There will be plenty of times that you are busy, stressed, or tired and just want to get something done. Take the extra time anyway, instead of half-assing your client interactions. It always comes back to you in a positive way.

The people who are successful are head-down working on their craft and their platform, while the folks phoning it in are regarded as irrelevant. If you want to generate good word-of-mouth about your business, you can't half-ass it, and you can't bail. If you commit to something, get it done. If you commit to playing a show, suck it up and play the show. Having to get up early the next day isn't a valid excuse to bail at the last minute. Fat Mike played an entire set on a couch after he'd thrown out his back. Thrice played an acoustic set at Warped Tour because the drummer had thrown out his back (touring is apparently bad for your back). I once shot a wedding with pneumonia, on top of Lyme disease. I've shot sick, I've shot injured. I shot on the day my dad had a heart attack (after I checked on him in the hospital, obviously. I'm not a monster). I've worked when I had what most people would consider completely valid reasons to cancel. But cancelling can be poisonous to your business, much like it is to a small, new band. Every time that band cancels a show at the last minute, that's one less promoter or one less venue that wants to work with it. That's one less kid who gives a shit when that band comes back to town. This is the exact opposite of what you want. If a band half-asses a show, it gets around. Sometimes, you get only one shot with people. *Yeah, I saw that band three years ago, they were terrible. I'm not going to that show.* Most of the business that I get is by word of mouth, and if I drop the ball, it gets around. People talk (and they tell two friends, then they tell two friends, then they tell the Internet . . .) it can be an exponential number of people who aren't going to give you a chance now. Thanks to the Internet, people have a huge platform to complain about your shoddy product or your terrible customer service. If you're not putting the effort in—even if it's *just this one time*—word can travel, and that's how people will view your business.

I'm always floored when people compliment me on how professional I am. It's not that I don't think I'm professional. It's that in these instances, I don't do anything above and beyond. I don't offer these clients some extraordinary service, I don't deliver beyond their wildest expectations. All I do is be nice and get the work delivered on time. That's it. Some people have been burned by lazy businesses before, though, and consider it a feat of greatness when you simply deliver something when you said you would. This is also why a simple apology when you have screwed up—when you under-delivered, went over the deadline, or forgot to return a phone call—goes a long way. People are used to cable companies' not showing up during the installation window and never apologizing for it, or airlines' cancelling flights and shrugging when asked, *well what do I do now?* Lazy businesses are making your job easier. Just meeting those basic expectations can make your customers raving, crazy happy. So can you imagine how excited they'd be if you *did* go above and beyond? If you exceeded those expectations? You'd have yourself some devoted Juggalos. Set your bar higher.

DON'T HALF-ASS IT.

WE LIVE OUR LIVES ANOTHER WAY

Being involved in a DIY culture offered me a different perspective on the type of work I did and on how I did it. If you didn't grow up listening to bad grindcore bands in VFW halls, never fear, there are plenty of other ways to seek out interesting worldviews. Traveling, reading, even just shifting the type of content you regularly consume can open up your worldview. It was hugely beneficial for me to meet people who lived differently from me in ways that I might not have imagined possible. I met people with work and hobbies that were outside of what I saw day-to-day, who came from different cultures, who had different viewpoints on how to get things done.

All the skills that kids learned in basements and in tour vans are being used now to start their businesses and NPOs. The skills kids learned while making zines and starting bands are transferable to an office setting. These people are willing to be clever, to figure out how to do more with less, to work around obstacles, and they're making it work. They've built their lives in a way that suited them.

No one knows how to live your life better than you. When people talk about the punk scene, it's often about breaking rules and railing against the man and anarchy and whatnot. The point isn't just to break rules, but to take a more thoughtful look at them. Not everything about existing systems is terrible, so keep the parts that serve you and work around the ones that don't. You question the way these things work. You look at your life and see if it makes sense or if there's a better way to go about it. The idea is to live consciously instead of making decisions by default. Momentum is a powerful force, and it's a lot easier to keep going to your day job, keep sending out the same newsletter updates to the same people, or keep saying *I'll start tomorrow*. It's easier, more comfortable to live the way you've been living. It's harder, but worthwhile, to take a look at why you're doing something and decide if you want to keep doing it. Because the nature of distribution is changing, because industries are evolving all the time, there are areas that just don't have rules yet. You get to make up your own.

A professor of mine started the design program at my school when he was hired. We didn't have a design program before then, and since there was no curriculum in place, he got to make it up. He could create the program how he wanted, because there wasn't any precedent, no *this is how we've always done it* to contend with. *This is how we've always done it* is a dangerous phrase used to end discussions or any further thought on the matter. At the time, the old way may have been the best way, but circumstances may have changed. There may be new methods available now that weren't around when we decided how a thing was done. It's important to stay open to the idea of revisiting decisions and processes. Maybe the way you've been doing it isn't the best course of action anymore. *This is how we've always done it* isn't going to help you accomplish anything new or interesting.

When I was looking for an internship in college, I cold-called 100 different agencies around town. I'm not exaggerating that point, literally, I called 100 agencies. One agency asked to get back to me, and I found out later it was because the company had never had a design intern before. The team could have just told me *no, we don't have design interns.* They didn't have any sort of routine as far as what kind of work an intern would do or what sort of hours one would keep. They hadn't done it before, and there was no system in place. Instead of saying no, they took a little bit of time to think about it. *Could we use an intern? Would we be able to offer something worthwhile? If we did hire an intern, how would we handle that?* They decided that it was worthwhile to try it out, and they hired me as their guinea pig. I mean intern. We got to create a plan that worked for them and for me, and they've continued to offer design internships every summer. You can look at doing something that no one has done before and be afraid because there aren't rules or any kind of guidance. Or you can look at something that no one has done before and think, *I can do this however I want to.*

Scott Smith, owner of East End Brewing Company, had been working as a mechanical engineer, a job that is unrelated to beer making. He'd had some experience brewing, as a hobby, and a family that embraced a DIY ethic, so when he quit a job that wasn't working for him, he looked to the beer landscape in Pittsburgh. Scott asked, *who's making beer around here?* and it turned out there weren't any places making craft beer, only brew pubs (which are basically also restaurants) and mass-production places. He saw a hole in the market that he could fill. But there's a lot of planning that goes into starting a brewery, and it's definitely one of those businesses that can't be started out of a home office.

Scott set out to rent an industrial-zoned space for less than $1,000 per month and to purchase equipment without going into debt, by spending only what he already had in savings. A few brew pubs had closed the year before he started the business, and he was able to buy their equipment. Having only ever brewed five gallons at a time, though, he'd never used this kind of gear, so he took photos of the setup to use as a guide to reassemble them in his own space. Scott set up a laptop on a bucket so that he could view the photos and put all the equipment back together in probably the most tedious way possible. And Scott made beer. Really good beer. But even great beer doesn't sell itself, so he started out by walking up and down Carson Street (which likely has the highest concentration of bars per square foot in the city), offering samples and trying to get distribution in bars. It took a lot of door-slamming to get a yes, but enough places agreed to sell East End beer that the business could get off the ground. Originally, Scott would show up with new kegs at the drop of a hat, but he soon realized why most breweries don't do this. Again, sometimes existing systems have solid reasoning behind them. Not grouping deliveries together was really inefficient and not very green (sustainability is an important value to Scott).

After running the brewery by himself for some time—beer making, cleaning, selling, delivery, web maintenance, marketing—the very first employee East End hired was a distributor. It eventually expanded to sell growlers (which is how you pick up craft beer on the go), and Scott found that they not only made a good margin on sales but also better engaged customers. People would have to physically come to the brewery to pick up the growlers (or later, to a storefront location) and would talk to the people that brewed East End, spawning the "don't buy beer from strangers" line. These days, East End Brewery employs eight people, and they're all more than happy to talk to you about beer. The storefront also helped to diversify the business, splitting income between direct and distributed sales. As the business grew, Scott was able to see what made sense to keep doing himself and what to delegate to someone else. He worked within existing systems when it served him and did things his own way when it didn't. And he met his goal of creating a sustainable, local brewery without going into debt to do it.

Having a different perspective means seeing another way to solve a problem. This is a huge benefit to companies that have real diversity in their workforces. If you gather people who have the same information, the same background, the same life experiences, the same inspiration, then you're going to get the same results. There's a lesser likelihood of hearing *but what if we tried it THIS way?* Einstein says, "We can't solve problems by using the same kind of thinking we used when we created them." Problem solving often requires a fresh perspective or an outside point of view. You may have too small a business to cultivate diversity within your workforce, but you can work to find new input channels to diversify your own thinking.

I don't want to pick on Pinterest or Instagram, or any number of other similar sites where you can showcase your work. They're cool sites, and you can build a great community on them, and let's face it, I'm on them too. But they're common to many industries. Say an illustrator is sitting at home, thinking about a piece she's working on, and maybe she looks at a popular Pinterest board for inspiration. She wants to make the kind of work that'll get onto that popular page, so she creates something that's inspired by those pieces. Someone else gets inspired by that illustrator's piece, which looks like those other pieces, and then makes a piece that looks like that other piece, and it turns into a circle jerk in which everything looks the same. There's always work that stands out, even on those curated popular pages, but that original work sits in a huge sea of copycats. You can see the same thing happen with apps (developers see what does well on app stores, they make similar things with similar-looking icons, and so on) and Kickstarter projects (things that get funded are similar to projects that have done well in the past). Every industry has its community showcase where the popular work lives. It's important to keep up with what's going on in your industry, but it's also important not to homogenize your input completely. Getting ideas from a variety of sources is the best way to make sure that you don't.

Routine input leads to routine output, so putting yourself into situations that you haven't been in before is great for inspiration. I took a class in college on sign language and Braille. I didn't have any good reason, it just seemed like an interesting class to me. My friends, who are maybe smarter than I am in this regard, mostly used their free credits in a concentrated area and earned a minor. I, instead, took anything that sounded remotely interesting to me—literature, ballet, Roman history, chemistry, whatever I could get into, and, of course, that sign-language class. A few semesters later, I ended up designing a logo for a communications company that used Braille. Because I'd had that class, because I'd been exposed to Braille, I had that connection somewhere in my brain. It's why I love getting on my soap box to support interdisciplinary education—it helps you to make interesting connections.

In addition to new experiences and subjects, expose yourself to new formats and media. Look outside your own industry for inspiration. If you're an illustrator, watch films. If you're a sports trainer, you can look to ballet for some new strength-training moves. If you bake elaborate and beautiful cakes, study architecture. For our honors program in college, we had something called centerpiece courses every semester. You'd have to create a project that would connect that centerpiece course with another class you were taking. Mostly, people wrote papers, but I tried to find more interesting opportunities. I combined a chemistry class with photography by making a cyanotype; algebra and scientific theory by building a ramp to teach Tartaglia's work on ballistics.

You can pool ideas not only to create work but also to market and promote it from some very unlikely sources. If your work is seasonal, you can look at marketing tactics from wedding photographers, construction companies, or ski instructors. It may not be specific to your industry, but those businesses tackle similar problems in advertising their work and managing cash flow. If you sell fitness trackers, look at companies that sell luxury beauty products or running shoes. You can learn just as much from companies that aren't like yours as you can from studying your own industry. If your market is overcrowded, try looking for customers that might benefit from what you're doing in an unexpected way. There are some weird intersections to be found, and the more sources you're exposed to, the bigger your pool is to pull from.

The goal is to put out work that's unique to you, to avoid creating a business that's exactly like a thousand others. When you offer the same thing, in the same way as dozens of other businesses, how do you market that? Price becomes the only competition point, and most people don't envision their businesses as a race to the bottom. The cover of *Wired* doesn't feature people talking about how they wanted their startups to be the cheapest. So figure out what's unique about your business, either in what you're offering or how you're offering it.

In addition to differentiating yourself from other businesses, you also want to watch out for falling into a rut. As a photographer, I've found myself leaning on the same compositions, repeating them with multiple clients. You find a thing that works, you get busy, and you keep doing just that thing that works. Don't get too comfortable in whatever it is that you're doing. I'm not saying that you should make a habit of throwing out everything you've done and starting over, but at least be open to the idea of discarding your loyalty to the work you've already done. Be willing to stretch. For me, I may not entirely abandon those compositions—they work well, and clients like them. But now, that's my base level. I expect to get those, so what else am I doing? What's the more creative shot that I'm going to try now?

I'm always setting personal goals for shoots, but I also need to recognize that those goals will continually change. Musicians frequently have to deal with backlash no matter what they do—either they're rehashing the same old sound and fans are mad or they've made too big a departure from what they've done before and fans are mad. Since they're going to be mad either way, you may as well be open to starting something completely new and different from what you've done before. Maybe right now, you're making a lot of

posters and t-shirts. But maybe in a few years, you'll mostly be doing album art or will have switched gears to working in the theater industry, or maybe we'll all have jet packs. It's great to have a five- or ten-year plan, but the future is not set in stone, and you can't necessarily know where your business will take you. You don't have to do what you do now forever. You may build on past work in ways that you didn't see coming when you started, and it's never

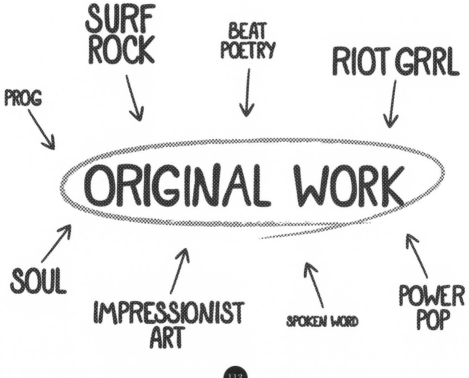

too late to change the path that you're on. It's important to revisit your goals, to check back in and see if you still want them. Continually asking these questions can help keep you on track. Is this new venture going to get me where I want to go, and is that still where I want to go?

Spending time around people who were working outside traditional structures helped to redefine my idea of success, as well. You get to have your own opinion of what makes you successful, because success looks like different things to different people. Ian MacKaye has said that success, for him, is in the doing of something. So when he first started playing bass, he considered that a success. His band wrote a song, a fantastic success. They played a show, and are deeply successful. For him, if he tried and he accomplished the thing he set out to do, that was success. It's incredibly easy to compare yourself to other businesses and start to feel like an abject failure because you don't have the things that they do. But you need to spend some time defining what a successful business looks like to you. Is it a certain amount of money you pull in? Is it being able to pursue your venture full-time? One person's view of success may be the ability to carve out two days a week to work on personal projects, and another's may be to work full-time at it and be able to support a family financially. Those two people have nothing to gain from comparing their businesses, because they have wildly different goals. Instead of measuring your success against other people, measure it against your goals and where you want to be.

HAVE SOME AUDACITY

I've saved what's arguably the most important bit for last. The TL;DR of the book (that's "too long; didn't read" for those of you that spend your time on worthwhile endeavors or going outside instead of reading Internet message boards). I talked a lot about shifting your perspective, building your network, finding your people, and putting out work that you're proud of. But none of that's helpful if you aren't able to get out and do the thing—to ship your product, to offer that class, to open a business. Getting out of the planning stage and into the getting-it-done stage is what makes you an entrepreneur instead of a person with a cool idea who is sort of thinking about maybe pursuing it one day.

When I started writing this section, it was originally called "Have Some Balls." But it's such a gendered expression, and, anyway, I get to say "balls" all the time, but I rarely get to throw around the word audacity. You can use whatever works for you, though—courage, cojones, chutzpah, general badassery. Whatever that thing is that helps you take a scary step, that's the thing you need. You're aiming for that sweet spot between imposter syndrome (in which you're entirely qualified but don't believe you are) and the Peter Principle (in which you're tasked with things you're absolutely not qualified to do). You need a healthy level of confidence in your abilities while still challenging yourself regularly.

There's an overwhelming message in the punk community that *you can do this, too*. If you have something to say and can knock out a few chords, then you have everything you need to start a band. When bands weren't touring through DC, bands started springing up in DC to create a local scene and word spread across the country. It wasn't always a matter of having talent, but they had the audacity to get up and do it. It's not easy to get up on stage and scream into microphones in front of your audience. At least if I make something that someone on the Internet hates, I don't have to stand there and watch them hate it. No one can chuck beer cans at me through the Internet. Punks don't wait for permission. They get up and say what they have to say without any real shield to protect them. And that takes guts. Now, I'm not saying that it isn't important for you to be skilled at what you do, because there's a difference between starting a project for fun and starting a business for profit. If you expect to make a living at something, you should probably be pretty good at it. What I mean is that you may be better at it than you're giving yourself credit for. You may have more than enough to start right now. You may not need the equipment or the resources that you think you do in order to get started.

When that metal band I talked about before, Name Withheld, talked to people, they said they were a bar band, because that's what they spent most of their time being. It's no surprise, then, when that's what people hired them to do. They communicated that they played bar music—with their words and with their presence in the same bar every weekend, playing that kind of music. If you don't believe in what you're doing (or in what you really want to be doing) enough to say so, why would anybody else? It's hard to turn down work that isn't right for you, especially if you really need the work. But you have to consider where you want to go with this thing that you're doing and whether this one job is taking you toward that goal or further away from it. Is this something I want people to know that I do? Does this action support what I keep saying I do?

It takes courage to get out there and say *this is what I'm doing*. It takes even more to keep saying that when the going gets rough. But it's important to own what you do, to be able to speak up and tell other people who you are. If one person says, *I'm a filmmaker*, and another says, *Oh, well, I'm a waiter but I do a little bit of film work sometimes, it's not a big deal*—who would you hire? The one who sounds capable, right? The one who says with confidence that he's a filmmaker. The one who sounds like a professional who knows what he wants. Plus, if you say, *I'm a filmmaker*, you may hear, *Oh, my friend has a script and she's looking for people to work with her on getting it made* . . . Maybe it's a style that you do, or maybe it's something you can refer to a friend. But if you say, *I'm a waiter but* . . . the conversation doesn't go that way, and you never get that information. People hire you for the sort of work they see you doing or the type of work you say that you do. They aren't psychic. They don't know that even though you're folding t-shirts at a retail space or working for an accounting firm right now, what you really want to do is start your own computer-repair shop. You need to tell them, and you need to show them. And you need to say it like you mean it.

Often the biggest hardship is starting. Taking that first step means that you need to start considering yourself as the type of person you want to be. I generally don't support being unprepared, but there is such a thing as too much research. I watched a commencement speech by author Neil Gaiman, and he said that people who know what they're doing know what's impossible. Whereas, people who don't know what they're doing,

"We were contacted to perform a benefit show for a fallen officer, which we agreed to since we didn't mind donating our time for a good cause. So once the show got closer we were given some more details, and they said not to worry about bringing anything but guitars and cymbals. Now, we're usually weird about that kind of thing, but we also had our annual Thanksgiving Eve show planned for that night so we decided *screw it*, that'll save us a ton of work loading and unloading. Fast forward to the night of, we show up shortly before we're supposed to go on because it was an earlier set time, plus we figured since we had no equipment to set up, what's the sense in getting there early? We walk in and immediately notice it's a much older crowd than our music usually appeals to, but again it's a benefit, so we had no idea what to expect. Needless to say we're kinda nervous at this point because we're pretty sure they won't enjoy what they hear. Around this point, we look to the stage and happen to notice there's one Marshall half stack, which is great, but then we look to the other amp, which happens to be a fender reverb amp, totally clean, no distortion-type amp. Basically, we're screwed. Everything we play (for the shortened, in-your-face set we prepared) needs distortion and since all our equipment was set up at the other venue, we didn't even have any pedals. So we decided that since I play most of the rhythm parts, I should use the Marshall, while our lead guitar player would be stuck with a nice smooth clean sound for all of his very punk solos and leads. We all joke about this horror of a show to this day. We learned a lot from that whole experience, and since then, we've always brought our own equipment to every show—even if we don't end up needing it, at least it's there. And while we've done a lot more benefits since then (some good, some bad), we've tried to make sure that the people asking us to perform understand exactly what they're getting, since it's better for everyone involved. No one wants to hear music they don't like, and, even more so, I don't want to force my music on unsuspecting people. Well, lesson(s) learned, I guess!"

—Reggie Little, August Ruins

don't. It's that punk-rock staple—form a band first, learn to play instruments later. It can be easier to do something when you don't know that it's ridiculous and impossible, and a bit of naive optimism can work in your favor. Besides, at a certain point, you're pencil sharpening. You have everything you need to get started except the audacity to take the leap. Stop procrastinating under the guise of research or planning, and recognize when your project is ready to get kicked out of the nest and start existing out in the world.

Part of the fear of speaking up about what you do is feeling like you don't have the experience. The first few times that someone asked me if I were a professional photographer, I hesitated. What does that even mean? Have I done enough shoots or earned enough money to say I am? All my tax forms say that I am, does that count for something? There isn't a rubric or some outside authority that can declare you a professional. And honestly, that's not what those people were asking me. They just wanted to know if they could hire me and know that I'd show up and get the job done, and that's a question I can definitely answer. Still, it takes some practice saying it out loud—audacity can be a learned skill, and the more you act like the sort of person that has that courage, the more you become a person that has it.

Fear of failure is another thing that keeps people from taking that big step and making their businesses official. You may fail at things along the way. Despite your planning, research, and getting up the courage to take a step, things don't always go according to plan. You're going to make mistakes if you're doing anything worthwhile. Anything that's successful was preceded by plenty of mistakes and failed prototypes, so at least make interesting mistakes. The idea is not to let the fear of failure keep you from ever doing anything. Things will go wrong, and no matter how hard you try, you can't be prepared for every single terrible thing that might happen. Go do it anyway.

Failure isn't always the worst thing that can happen, as it turns out, and failure can make you braver. Most of the time when you do fail, you look around and realize that it didn't kill you. It didn't bankrupt your entire business. Maybe nothing that terrible happened. The next time you take a scary step, the prospect of failure will be less terrifying.

What if people don't like what I put out there? Well . . . what if they don't? What's the worst that can happen? Each step I took toward growing a business was a little easier, because I'd taken scary steps before and survived. Comedians talk about the power of bombing—once, anyway, there's no need to make a habit of it. That's always the fear, that you'll get up there, and the whole audience will hate you. Or worse, they will be completely indifferent and bored, and you bomb. Then you walk offstage, you're not dead, and you've got another gig in a few days. Life sort of goes on. Failure is no longer the worst thing that could happen. So when you get that bigger gig, for a larger crowd, you think *What's the worst that could happen? I'm gonna bomb? I've already done that, what can they do to me now?* You can become more confident in your ability to do things simply by doing them. Over and over again.

I learned a lot from failing, but maybe calling it trial and error sounds more generous. If I got burned on a contract, I knew to add in something that protected me for the next one. Having a client that didn't pay an invoice taught me to require a deposit. Working with couples that weren't a good fit taught me that I could—and should—turn down some jobs. I didn't know everything about running a business when I started one, but with every job, every client, I learned something new.

I grew up with the type of dad who values knowledge over experience when it comes to taking on projects. *I've never done that before* wasn't considered a valid excuse not to do something. He decided to build a living room as an addition onto our house, which meant digging out the space, pouring cement for the foundation of the basement, building out the room and roof, and doing the wiring, all of it. I said, "have you ever built a room before?" He said, "No, but I have a book." Oh. A book. That guy has audacity in spades. And to his credit, it's the most well-constructed room of that house (and, point of fact, the only truly level one).

Sometimes when I tell that story, people think it's batshit insanity to take on a project like that without having the experience of doing it before. But just because he's never done that specific thing doesn't mean that he isn't qualified to do so. He's worked with power tools and concrete before, on much smaller projects. He's excellent at math. His reading comprehension is such that he can follow basic tenets of construction laid out in a book. He has acquired skills over his life that can be applied to this project, even though it's the first time he's done this. Maybe you haven't started a business before, so you think you're not qualified to do it now. But there are other ways to acquire the skills you need to succeed, and you may already have a lot of them. If I can learn them from hanging around kids sporting Aus Rotten patches in dingy basements, surely you can find some applicable experiences in your own life.

So much of what I've learned, what I know how to do now, came out of projects in which I had the ideas first and figured out the logistics later. I learned how movie clips in Flash worked because I thought it was exceptionally important that my animated character kept blinking while he waited for you to press the "next" button. I learned how to storyboard and plan a film shoot because I had to complete a film for my master's thesis (with about only six months to make it happen and no large-scale-film-production experience to speak of). And my first real salaried position was not a position that I was really all that qualified for. I was hired as a webmaster for a medium-sized hospital. I'd coded my own sites before and could do pretty basic things, but handling a big corporate website and intranet with dynamic content was not in my wheelhouse. If the company had asked if I'd done that kind of work before, I would have had to say no. But instead, I was asked if I could do it, which is an entirely different question. And yes, absolutely, I can do that. I got the job, and learned a lot, and absolutely nothing terrible happened to anyone.

During his speech Neil Gaiman spoke about a friend of his who'd also been hired to a position that she wasn't exactly qualified for. His advice to her was to pretend that she was the sort of person who could do that. Fake it 'til you make it, or, rather, fake it 'til you realize you were actually pretty well-qualified to do this thing after all. I didn't take on a job as a heart surgeon or something, Frank-Abagnale-style. I took on a job, having reason to believe I could do well, even though I didn't have the experience to prove it. Eventually, I discovered that a lot of people felt that way about their work, and if you're ever looking to move your way up in a company, at some point, it means taking on work that's new to you.

It's failing up. Failing toward something better, and eventually gaining ground. It's working through whatever obstacle is in front of you. Sometimes you get in your own way, thinking that you aren't good enough or that you need some kind of outside permission to do what you want. But you can build your life the way that you want to. You're allowed to take a look at your life and decide if what you're doing makes sense or if there's a better way to do it. You're allowed to question if you're living this way because that's just what you're supposed to do, because of momentum in that direction, or because that's the best way to do it. Living in a conscious way means asking why we do things the way we do them. Having audacity means being willing to do it differently. If you still feel like you need someone's permission, then, hey, you have mine. It's in a book, which makes it super official. So write your awful lyric, take your awful photo, because some terrible things are stepping stones to better things. Some okay things eventually transform into good things. Start. If you have something to say, something to offer, put it out there, because no one is stopping you. Put your whole heart into it, and own what you do. Have some audacity.

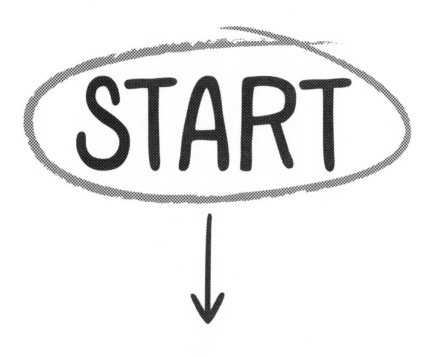

Some thank yous are in order.

To John Moore, for supporting me through making a book and a baby in the same year. A lesser man would have run away screaming years ago.

To my parents, who raised me to be like this.

To Joseph Hughes, Jeff Finley, and Jonathan Kahn for giving me space on their stages to work out these thoughts, and to everyone that showed up to hear them.

To Shannon Sankey and Luke McDermott for making me sound like a real writer.

To Rob Carney, for suggesting I write this thing in the first place.

To everyone that ever let me crash on their couch, floor, or spare bed. To everyone that hired me to take their photo or draw their nonsense.

To Elly Blue, Joe Biel, and the whole Microcosm team for making this happen, and for being so supportive through the whole process.

To Adam Joad, Curtis Sproul, Scott McMaster II, Scott Smith, Evie Bagwell, Dan Cassaro, David Wilson, Jason Chandler, Dan Rock, Becki Hollen, and Reggie Little for sharing their stories.

Finally, to my son. I hope you pull all of this nonsense, and then some.

RESOURCES

Things I talked about, and where you can find them:

You can find my design work at **MooreDesign.us** and wedding photography work at **MooreClick.com**.

Bands:

DOA // facebook.com/doapunk
DRI // dirtyrottenimbeciles.com
Rogue Wave // facebook.com/roguewave
Flatline // flatline.iwarp.com
The Replacements // thereplacementsofficial.com
Scattered Hamlet // scatteredhamlet.com
Henry Rollins // henryrollins.com
Campfire Conspiracy // campfireconspiracy.bandcamp.com
Signals Midwest // signalsmidwest.tumblr.com
Worship This! // worshipthis.tumblr.com
Anti-Flag // anti-flag.com
Skies Bleed Black // purevolume.com/skiesbleedblack
Bobby Joe Ebola and the Children MacNuggits // bobbyjoeebola.com
The Ramones // seriously? Google them.
Thrice // thrice.net
World's Scariest Police Chases // worldsscariestpolicechases.com
The Frustrators // facebook.com/thefrustrators
ICP // insaneclownposse.com

Bastard Bearded Irishmen // bastardbeardedirishmen.com

August Ruins // facebook.com/augustruins

Green Day // greenday.com

Events & Venues:

Dare Conf // 2014.dareconf.com

Weapons of Mass Creation Fest // wmcfest.com

924 Gilman Street Project // 924gilman.org

The Fest // thefestfl.com

ABC No Rio // abcnorio.org

The Mr. Roboto Project // therobotoproject.org

Artists:

Joe McNally // portfolio.joemcnally.com

David Hobby // strobist.blogspot.com

Dan Cassaro // youngjerks.com

Larry Livermore // larrylivermore.com

Brandon Rike // brandonrike.com

Winston Smith // winstonsmith.com

Louis CK // louisck.net

Jason Chandler // facebook.com/horriblecomics

Everyday Balloons // everydayballoonsshop.com

Neil Gaiman // neilgaiman.com

Zines, etc:

Maximum Rocknroll // maximumrocknroll.com

Book Your Own Fucking Life // byofl.org

Punk Globe // punkglobe.com

Projects, Businesses, and other Cool Shit

East End Brewery // eastendbrewing.com

Bike Pittsburgh // bikepgh.org

Agents of Change Recycling // facebook.com/agentsofchangerecyling

50 and 50 // statemottosproject.com

Ferocious Quarterly // fe.rocious.com

Commonwealth Press // cwpress.com

Deeplocal // deeplocal.com

Firefly // usually running in marathon format on the Scifi channel

Tech Shop // techshop.ws

Go Media // gomedia.com

Pittsburgh City Paper // pghcitypaper.com

Giant Eagle // gianteagle.com

In the Blood Tatoo // inthebloodtattoo.com

Record Labels:

Tiny Engines // tinyengines.net

Epitaph Records // epitaph.com

Alternative Tentacles // alternativetentacles.com

Dischord Records // dischord.com

SUBSCRIBE TO EVERYTHING WE PUBLISH!

Do you love what Microcosm publishes?

Do you want us to publish more great stuff?

Would you like to receive each new title as it's published?

Subscribe as a BFF to our new titles and we'll mail them all to you as they are released!

$10-30/mo, pay what you can afford. Include your t-shirt size and month/ date of birthday for a possible surprise! Subscription begins the month after it is purchased.

microcosmpublishing.com/bff

...AND HELP US GROW YOUR SMALL WORLD!

Read more about Punk Rock Empowerment: